An Invitation to Love:
Lessons in Living

by Lydia K. Shifman

faithAlivebooks
Grand Rapids, Michigan

An Invitation to Love: Lessons in Living
Copyright © 2008 Lydia Schifman and faithAlivebooks
All rights reserved.

No part of this book may be reproduced or used in any form without written permission from the publisher.

ISBN 0-9764221-1-5

Requests for information should be addressed to:
faithAlivebooks.com
491 Prestwick Dr. S.E.
Grand Rapids, MI 49546

Interior design by Kate Budzynski
Cover design by Bob Lizza

faithAlivebooks
Grand Rapids, Michigan

To my three grandsons,
　　　Brendon, Eric and Ryan

TABLE OF CONTENTS

Acknowledgments
Foreword
Introduction

PART ONE: FROM THE OLD TESTAMENT
1. Abraham, Sarah and Hagar
2. The Testing Of Abraham
3. The Call Of Moses
4. The Exodus
5. The Ten Commandments
6. The Ratification Of The Covenant
7. The Book Of Ruth
8. Solomon's Judgment
9. Out Of The Whirlwind
10. The Story Of Tobit
11. The Book Of Esther

PART TWO: FROM THE NEW TESTAMENT
12. Mother of God
13. The Visitation
14. The Presentation
15. The Holy Family
16. The Baptism Of Jesus
17. A Lesson From The Beloved
18. The Call To Faith
19. The Transfiguration
20. The Agony In The Garden
21. The Way Of The Cross
22. The Empty Tomb
23. The Martyrdom Of Stephen
24. The Church Is Born
25. The Blessed Sacrament
26. The Call To Witness
27. Who Do You Say I Am?

PART THREE: THE CALL TO PRAYER
28. God Is Listening
29. What Is God Asking Of You?
30. In The Darkness There Is Light
31. Rachel's Children
32. In Celebration Of A Life
33. The Tree Of Life

Epilogue
Glossary Of Terms
End Notes

"Come to me, all you that yearn for me and be filled with my fruits; You will remember me as sweeter than honey, better to have than the honeycomb."
Sirach 24: 18,19

An Invitation to Love: Lessons in Living

by Lydia K. Shifman

Acknowledgements

This spiritual journal evolved over a period of five years. During that time I was gifted with the help of many wonderful people. I am especially grateful to *Sister Jo Louise Magdalinski OSF* for her ever-present support, preparation of the manuscript, for literally opening doors for its publication and for her gift of friendship, which is treasured; to *Sister Pacelli OSF* for her critique of the manuscript and for writing the Forward; to *Sister Margaret Kolb OCD* my Spiritual Guide; to *Sister Angela Pikus OCD* for previewing the manuscript and for her insight and assistance in editing; to *The Carmelite Nuns of Elysburg, Pa.* for their prayers and wishes which reflect the beauty and fruit of their Carmelite vocation; to *Dr. John Dennehy and his wife, Idita,* for the use of their personal library; to *Dr. John O'Rourke and his wife, Nancy,* and members of *The St. Joseph Charismatic Prayer Group, St. Joseph's Church, Danville, Pa.—Dee Pitko, Joyce Delaney, Don and Helen Miller, Lou and Anne Piestrak, Elaine Mirarchi, Ellen Goretsky* and *Lou* and *Kathy Dalton* for the ability to share sections of the manuscript in the form of teachings; to *Dr. Cathy Wallace,* my first Cursillo mentor, who "charged me" to begin the journal and to members of my *Cursillo Group, St. Joseph's Church, Danville, Pa.— Roseanne Quick, Bernadine Markey, Lorraine Burke, Maureen Hill, Dianne Carrier, Mary Anne Hackenberg, and Peggy Dimmick* for their support; to *Ellen Matragrano* for aptly coining my little drawings as "symbolic representations of the Word; to *Mary Anise* for her personal reflections of the drawings; to *Leah Morton, Lenore Miller* and *Evelyn Morris* who demonstrated for me that the manuscript provides a virtual experience for the reader and can be a vehicle for religious tolerance and unity; to *Dan Pierson* for believing in the manuscript; to *Bob Lizza* for his graphic reproductions of the drawings and to…

St. Therese of Liseux, for Her Little Way.

Foreword

Indeed this book is, as the author says, "an invitation to love." It is an invitation that was answered in many ways while the work was in progress. It draws upon the many faceted career of its author in its attempt to reach out to a diverse population that is searching for spiritual roots.

Writing about the call to holiness is always a difficult task because the idea of being "holy" seems, for many, to mean being extraordinary. Yet that is far from the truth. As Christians, by our Baptism, we are called to walk with Christ toward a goal which can only be reached by those who become holy. It is a call not merely for those consecrated to religious life because all who are baptized are "called." This call is an expression of a human desire to be the very best—the most perfect—individual that one can be, according to the faith that illuminates and reflects this ideal perfection.

Furthermore, if we believe in Divine providence and God's care for us, we need to accept the circumstances of our lives that shape our path to Him and that gives us the means to bring others to Him. This fact is very well illustrated by the way that Lydia Shifman has drawn upon her life experiences as inspiration for this work. These life experiences embrace those from her career fields of social work, healthcare, pastoral care, counseling and even from a monastic experience. She has worked with a broad segment of society in these fields and has championed the needs of women, adolescents and children. She has taught, lectured, researched and written in a variety of disciplines.

The variety and diversity of these experiences are reflected in this book by her ability to focus on the heart of the story which she has chosen to contemplate and in her ability to communicate her thoughts in unique ways. Drawing upon her love of reading, she has been able to connect her thoughts to those of authors in many other literary and professional fields as well as to the inspiration found in Scripture. The reader will find that the structure of these readings presents a progressive format intended to draw the reader into interaction with the chosen passages. Meditating on these passages in this text should bring the reader to a deeper understanding of his or her faith, or at least to greater appreciation of the place of faith in daily life.

I would ask the reader to approach this book for what it is. It represents the thoughtful contemplation of one who has lived fully, prayed sincerely and often, and who now desires to share the fruits and blessings of this experience with her readers. If you enter into the spirit in which this book was written, I have no doubt that you will be changed because I believe that the Holy Spirit fills these pages with wisdom.

Sister M. Pacelli Staskiel, OSF, PhD
Professor, English/Communication
Academic Dean Emerita, Alvernia College

INTRODUCTION

This book is an invitation to enter into the sacred mystery of Love. It is an experiential spiritual journal. Wrapped in the practice of praying with scripture, this book is about stretching in God's love and becoming a measure of his dream, a holy people. It answers the universal call to be His Witness: to follow His Way. Bound in passages of sacred scripture, this journal holds a collection of reflections, symbolic representations of the Word and rich teachings from the great Saints, mystics and theologians. It is an invitation to walk in faith, pray with scripture and then capture its lessons.

In the wake of 9/11, I became a member of the Cursillo Movement. At that time I pledged to be a witness to the resurrection and life of our Lord Jesus Christ. Meeting thereafter with other members from my church, I was asked to present a plan for evangelization. I remember sharing I had no idea, other than to be myself: an older woman who loved God. Sometime later I took the question to prayer, seeking an answer through the ancient method of praying with scripture, Lectio Divina. It was not extraordinary that I would seek an answer to a life question through scripture. Twenty years earlier, after reading both the Old and New Testaments and in particular, The Four Gospels, I found the meaning of life and became a Believer. Ten years later, after attending a Mass, I found my home and became a Jewish convert to Catholicism.

I learned the ancient prayer form Lectio Divina during two extraordinary years living in a Carmelite Monastery. It was there I began to practice mental prayer while studying the spiritual traditions of St. Teresa of Avila. I also began to draw simple symbolic representations of the Sacred Word. Not until much later did I realize these little pictures were part of my prayer. Because I love to read and the fact that the Carmelites had a wonderful library, I had little difficulty becoming immersed in the writings of the Saints, mystics and theologians. There was much to learn and ever so much to pray about. With these precious gifts in mind, I told my Cursillo group I would begin to keep a record of both my scripture selections and reflections. This book is that journal. To my surprise it has become a vehicle for evangelization.

God calls each of us to holiness, which is a part of one's faith walk. By our baptism and confirmation we are chosen to be people of the "Covenant of Love" to become *living stones ... built into a spiritual house* (1 Pet 2-4). The call to holiness is the universal call to the Lay Apostolate.[1] Indeed, it is a call needing to be heard because there is a growing climate of spirituality in our world that appears to be without roots in traditional religious belief. St. Paul reminds us *...as you received Christ Jesus the Lord, walk in him rooted in him and built upon him ... established in faith. ... See to it that no one captivates you with an empty seductive philosophy according to human tradition ... and not according to Christ* (Col 2:6-8).

Yet, most of us are either turned off by the word "holy" or think of it as too difficult to achieve. Perhaps this feeling stems from misconceived ideas about holiness. Generally speaking, when we think about being holy, we attribute it to someone we view as being either very pious or enlightened. However, St. Paul also tells us *...as God's chosen ones holy and beloved, we need to put on heartfelt compassion, kindness, humility and patience, bearing with one another and forgiving one another. And over all these we are to put on love, that is, the bond of perfection* (Col 3:10, 12, 13, 14). This is what holiness is about. The simple truth is, love is not solely an activity of the heart, but is also of the will.[2] Holiness is about living out our lives girded in love. It is about living the virtues authentically, stumbling and even falling, yet still persevering. It is also about learning to accept the crosses in our lives. Indeed, we all stand naked in our vulnerability as we face the limits of our human condition and find, perhaps for the first time, the essence of what it means to surrender to His will. Trust does not come easily. Yet, holiness is about committed faith. It is about embracing the cross in the light of truth. Only within the mystery of grace can the self reach for that luminous source and find wholeness where there was brokenness. Only in abject humility can one's soul enter the streams of compassion that are enfolded within His cloak of peace.

PRAYING WITH SCRIPTURE

In the beginning was the Word
and the Word was with God
and the Word was God.
   John 1:1

Praying with scripture is a faith-building experience. It is an opportunity to "listen" to the Word of God.[3] Led by the Holy Spirit, the reader enters a sacred journey of love that transcends time. It is a life-giving experience that brings the living Word into one's daily life. Selecting scripture varies. It may occur as one listens to a Gospel reading or hears a sermon that touches the heart or leaves one feeling bewildered and wanting more. What counts is just beginning!

As stated above, I began this journal shortly after the horrific acts of violence that occurred on 9/11. Like everyone else, I was overwhelmed and decided I needed to understand why this could have happened. I began to pray to the Holy Spirit asking for help. One day, I decided to see if scripture held an answer. I reread the text about Abraham, Sarah and Hagar. Then I searched the Web for information regarding the concept of "the collective memory." Shortly thereafter, I read an article in the December 2001 issue of *National Geographic* about Abraham, the Father of Three Faiths. I was profoundly moved and decided it was time to write. This writing was the beginning of this book. With the exception of the writings on the martyrdom of St. Stephen, the Exodus and God is Listening, each scripture passage was chosen following a Gospel reading at Mass or after praying the Liturgy of the Hours. The most important part of my journey, however, occurred when I sought the assistance of a Spiritual Guide. I strongly recommend spiritual direction for those who choose to become actively engaged in the practice of Lectio Divina.

Praying with scripture is our opportunity to glean from its ancient stories and events lessons for living in today's world. "Scripture is one book with an inherent unity" and so it was natural for me to include readings from both the Old and New Testaments.[4] The purpose of Part Three, The Call to Prayer is to bring you, the reader, into the reality of our mutual need for God and God's need for us to become His holy people.

How To Use This Book

To pray to the Holy Spirit is to seek truth.
To pray for understanding is to learn what is hidden.
To pray for God's will ... is to follow His way.

Praying with scripture is an experiential process that involves one's intellect, body, heart and soul. Because of this fact, this book is to be utilized as a starting point for personal prayer and meditation. You need only bring to the process your attention, a journal and a pencil or pen. Settling into the silence is never easy, although lighting a candle and calling upon the Holy Spirit is a good way to begin. If you continue to find yourself distracted by thoughts or worries, take a moment to honor each and then share them with God. Know that each worry or distraction can become part of your prayer. He is just waiting for you to turn it over to Him.

My suggestion is that you then begin by reviewing the outline on Lectio Divina that can be found in the Glossary. Then *select for meditation any scripture passage from either Part One or Two*. Read it slowly. Jot down any lines or words that seem to grab your attention. Perhaps a thought has come up. Add that thought to your notes. Then move on to the illustration and repeat the process.

The drawings are simple symbolic representations of a heart that is centered in The Word. With the help of the Holy Spirit, one's imagination is enriched within the meditative process with the eye creating a visual memory that recognizes the Word as an endless circle of love. Each scripture image is a wordless prayer that acknowledges this gift with gratitude. As noted by Harrington, it is not unusual for creativity to evolve within the practice of Lectio Divina; it is to be encouraged.[5] So it is recommended after you read and meditate, you consider not only journaling, but also capturing your thoughts in poetry, music, song, dance or in art with its many wondrous forms including graphics, sculpture or photography. Know whatever you create need not be perfect. Rather, it need only be enjoyed and celebrated!

The reflections that follow each scripture reading are my conversations with God. Each represent afterthoughts arrived through continuous mental prayer, readings and deliberation. They characterize the unfolding of a heart that continuously seeks transformation recognizing its ever present need … regardless of one's age. Why not try writing a letter to God? Each becomes your prayer!

The readings are excerpts taken from the writings of Saints, mystics and theologians. They were used to both expand and reinforce my own personal thoughts. For me these fertile writings are divine breaths of inspirit love. Perhaps you will find a different reading that has special meaning for you. Why not include it in your journal?

What better way to end one's time in prayer than with *a psalm from the Psalter*? Each is an experiential response. Moreover the wonder and majesty of God is appreciated in the fullness of His glory. And so it follows that one ends this experience with thanksgiving and in the power of the "Amen."

At the end of each prayer episode, I included *a challenge*, which is in the form of questions. It is also important to note these questions can also form a foundation for discussion in small groups.

Now it is your time to journey into the Sacred.

Part One:
Lessons From The Old Testament

*"Glorify the Lord with me,
let us together extol His name."*
Psalm 34:4

Abraham, Sarah and Hagar

CLOCKWISE: *Count the stars; Sarah presents Hagar to Abraham; Hagar and her son Ishmael; Abraham offers hospitality and a message was given; Sarah bears Abraham a son named Isaac; Abraham sends Hagar and Ishmael into the desert; Isaac and Ishmael bury Abraham in the cave of Machpelah.*

Scripture

"Look up at the sky and count the stars, if you can. Just so ... shall your descendents be."
    Genesis 15:5

Sarai said to Abram: "The Lord has kept me from bearing children. Have intercourse, then, with my maid; perhaps I shall have sons through her."
    Genesis 16:2

Hagar bore Abram a son, and Abram named the son whom Hagar bore him Ishmael.
    Genesis 16:15

The Lord appeared to Abraham by the terebinth of Mamre, as he sat in the entrance of his tent while the day was growing hot. Looking up he saw three men standing nearby. When he saw them he ran ... to greet them; and bowing to the ground he said: "Sir if I may ask you this favor please do not go on past your servant. Let some water be brought that you may bathe your feet and then rest yourselves under the tree ... let me bring you a little food that you may refresh yourselves."
    Genesis 18:1-5

"Where is your wife Sarah?" they asked him. "There in the tent," he replied. One of them said, "I will surely return to you about this time next year, and then Sarah will have a son."
    Genesis 18:9, 10

The Lord took note of Sarah as he had said he would; he did for her as he had promised. Sarah became pregnant and bore Abraham a son in his old age, at the set time that God had stated.
    Genesis 21:1, 2

...Abraham sent (Hagar) away ... the water in the skin was used up. So she put the child down under a shrub, and then went and sat down opposite him. ... God heard the boy's cry and

God's messenger called to Hagar.
   Genesis 21:14-17

His sons Isaac and Ishmael buried (Abraham) in the cave of Machpelah ... next to his wife Sarah.
   Genesis 25:9, 10

Thoughts

Abba

O Jerusalem, city of God, a great schism exists within your walls. Winds of evil lurk everywhere, forming secret pockets of imploding violence all over our globe. Cries that mourn the dead also shout revenge until one can hardly hear the peacemakers.

Where did so much hatred and bitterness begin? It is as if over time our collective memory embedded by experiences of rejection, ethnic cleansing, abject hunger, genocide and war has twisted our souls to the point that we have become lost. Good seems to have disappeared and in its place is only hatred and bitterness. It is no wonder people seem willing to enter into the wrath of the warrior. It is no wonder their collective memory has difficulty accepting the concept of forgiveness. Retelling the stories of past persecutions without any measure of forgiveness only insures that the fabric of hatred that corrupts the soul will emerge into the present.[1]

You said to Abraham, "*I will make of you a great nation and I will bless you*" (Gen 12:2). "*Look up at the sky and count the stars if you can. Just so shall your descendents be*" (Gen 15:5). And so it was that Abraham became the grand patriarch of our Judeo-Christian heritage and of the Muslim world.

Despite this fact, many people are filled with long-held intergenerational feelings of mistrust. It is as if we are only united in our division. One cannot help but wonder as others did 2,000 years ago: *Where do the wars and where do the conflicts ... come from?* Then we are reminded: *Is it not from your passions that make war*? (James 4-1).

Two sons were born to Abraham. First Ishmael, whose mother Hagar was Abraham's concubine. His wife Sarah gave Hagar to Abraham because she was barren. Yet, you never forgot your covenant with Abraham. Sarah bore Abraham a son whom they called Isaac, although both were well beyond their childbearing years. Scripture also records that you blessed Ishmael, promising *he would become the father of twelve chieftains* (Gen 17:19-22). Yet, you maintained your covenant with Isaac.

Though both children were blessed, you affirmed Sarah's position as Abraham's wife and upheld Isaac's inheritance. You allowed Sarah to send Hagar and Ishmael into the wilderness, but sent an angel to ensure they would both survive. Because of Sarah's action both children were raised separately. Scripture also records that Abraham purchased a parcel of land in Canaan. Although Abraham purchased land that you promised the chosen people, it remains a land of division. When Sarah died she was buried in a cave in Keneath-arbat, which is today known as Hebron.

But what happened to the sons of Abraham and their descendents? Scripture tells us when Abraham died at the recorded age of 175 both sons, Isaac and Ishmael, buried him next to his wife, Sarah. Could it be that the sons of Abraham knew each other, even though they lived apart? A recent study of the DNA of male Jews and Middle Eastern Arabs, among them Syrians, Palestinians and Lebanese, indicate they share a common set of ancestors. These then are the descendents of Abraham, true friend of God.[2]

...As (Jesus) drew near, he saw the city (Jerusalem) and wept over it, saying "If this day you only knew what makes for peace—but now it is hidden from your eyes..." (Luke 19:41-42, 43).[3]

A Reading

The people are in confusion and cannot find rest,
An object of disdain and scorn:
It will be thus until the final battle.
But before the cross appears again in heaven,
Even before Elijah comes to gather his own,
The good Shepard goes silently through the land,

Now and then he gathers from the depths of the abyss
A little lamb shelters it at his heart.
And then others always follow him.
But there above the throne of grace
The Mother ceaselessly pleads for her people,
She seeks souls to help her pray.
Then only when Israel has found the Lord
Only then when he has received his own,
Will he come in manifest glory
And we must pray for this second coming.

The day of manifest glory,
When above the head of the Queen of Carmel
The crown of stars will gleam brilliantly.
Because the twelve tribes will have found their Lord.[4]

Psalm Response

I rejoiced because they said to me,
"We will go up to the house of the Lord."
And now we have set foot
within your gates. O Jerusalem
with compact unity.

To it the tribes go up,
the tribes of the Lord.
According to the decree for Israel,
to give thanks to the name of the Lord.
In it are set up judgment seats,
seats for the house of David.

Pray for the peace of Jerusalem!
May those who love you prosper!
May peace be within your walls,
prosperity in your buildings.
Because of my relatives and friends
I will say, "Peace be within you!"
Because of the house of the Lord,

our God,
I will pray for your good.
Amen.
    Psalm 122

THE CHALLENGE

Can you find within the scripture what God is trying to teach us? What is the lesson to be learned?

The Testing of Abraham

Clockwise: *Abraham is put to the test by God; Abraham puts the wood for the holocaust on Isaac's back; Isaac asks, "Where is the sheep for the holocaust?"; The altar is built and the Lord's messenger calls Abraham; A Ram is seen in the thicket.*

Scripture

... God put Abraham to the test. He called to him, "Abraham!" "Ready!" he replied. Then God said: "Take your son Isaac, your only one, whom you love, and go to the land of Moriah. There you shall offer him up as a holocaust on a height that I will point out to you." Early the next morning Abraham saddled his donkey, took with him his son Isaac, and two of his servants as well, and with the wood that he had cut for the holocaust, set out for the place of which God had told him.

On the third day Abraham got sight of the place from afar. Then he said to his servants: "Both of you stay here with the donkey, while the boy and I go over yonder. We will worship and then come back to you." Thereupon Abraham took the wood for the holocaust and laid it on his son Isaac's shoulders, while he himself carried the fire and the knife. As the two walked on together, Isaac spoke to his father Abraham. "Father!" he said. "Yes, son," he replied. Isaac continued, "Here are the fire and the wood, but where is the sheep for the holocaust?" "Son," Abraham answered, "God himself will provide the sheep for the holocaust." Then the two continued going forward.

When they came to the place of which God had told him, Abraham built an altar there and arranged the wood on it. Next he tied up his son Isaac, and put him on top of the wood on the altar. Then he reached out and took the knife to slaughter his son. But the Lord's messenger called to him from heaven, "Abraham, Abraham!" "Yes Lord," He answered. "Do not lay your hand on the boy," said the messenger. "Do not do the least thing to him. I know now how devoted you are to God, since you did not withhold from me your own beloved son." As Abraham looked about, he spied a ram caught by its horns in the thicket. So he went and took the ram and offered it up as a holocaust in place of his son.
    Genesis 22:1-19

THOUGHTS

Abba

You tested Abraham's faith and learned your friend was fully prepared to sacrifice his son, Isaac. Abraham understood obedience meant surrendering his will to you, whom he fiercely loved and trusted. As Abraham proved his filial and duty bound love, he also learned that your plan for Isaac was not bound in death, but rather in life. Abraham was called by you to be a father; your glory ... your offspring![1] Abraham learned that you do not *rejoice in the destruction of the living. For (you) fashioned all things that they might have being"* (Wis 1:13, 14).[2]

We, too, are called to be spiritually whole. To learn that loving you means seeking your will to be obedient and to rely on you with total trust. You ask each of us to direct our lives toward all that is life giving. This is your plan for humanity. The measure of your eternal love was the ultimate sacrifice of your beloved son Jesus, who died so that we would have the opportunity to be reconciled with you and find life even in death. "Abraham offered to God his mortal son who did not die, and God gave up his immortal Son who died for all of us."[3]

A READING

O Abraham, may you be blessed! Isaac, who so meekly allowed yourself to be bound to the altar, may you be blessed! My God, who makes such virtues spring for men, may you be blessed from age to age forever. Love means obeying you with this promptness and this faith, in ways that rend the heart and turn the mind upside down ... love is the immediate absolute sacrifice to your will and glory of what is most dear. ... It is what you did, in a wonderful way, O Abraham, getting up at once in the night to go to sacrifice your son. It is what you will do. O Son of God, coming from heaven to earth to live that life and die that death ... ! My Lord and my God, so may it be with me also, according to your most holy will.[4]

Psalm Response

Your ways, O Lord, make known to me;
teach me your paths.
Guide me in your truth and teach me
for you are God my savior
and for you I wait all day.
Good and upright is the Lord;
thus he shows sinners the way.
He guides the humble to justice,
he teaches the humble his way.
All the paths of the Lord are
kindness and constancy
Toward those who keep his
covenant and his decrees.
Amen.
      Psalm 25:4, 5, 8-10

The Challenge

Think about a time that either you, or someone you knew, chose simply to trust in God while knowing, to do so, would be at a personal sacrifice.

Have you ever had to stand-alone in order to remain true to your Christian values? How did your decision affect you?

The Call of Moses

Scripture

Meanwhile Moses was tending the flock of his father-in-law Jethro, the priest of Midian. Leading the flock across the desert, he came to Horeb, the mountain of God. There an angel of the Lord appeared to him in fire flaming out of a bush. As he looked on, he was surprised to see that the bush, though on fire, was not consumed. So Moses decided, "I must go over to look at this remarkable sight and see why the bush is not burned." When the Lord saw him coming over to look at it more closely, God called out to him from the bush "Moses! Moses!" He answered, "Here I am." God said, "Come no nearer! Remove the sandals from your feet. For the place where you stand is holy ground. I am the God of your father," he continued, "the God of Abraham, the God of Isaac, the God of Jacob." Moses hid his face for he was afraid to look at God. But the Lord said, I have witnessed the affliction of my people in Egypt and have heard their cry of complaint against their slave drivers, so I know well what they are suffering. Therefore, I have come down to rescue them from the hands of the Egyptians and lead them out of that land into a good and spacious land, a land flowing with milk and honey, the country of the Canaanites, Hittites, Amorites, Perizzites, Hivites and Jebusites. So indeed the cry of the Israelites has reached me, and I have truly noted that the Egyptians are oppressing them. Come now! I will send you to Pharaoh to lead my people, the Israelites, out of Egypt."
   Exodus 3:1-10

Thoughts

Abba

In the midst of tribulation you called Moses to be your intercessor, to liberate your chosen people, the Israelites. When Moses saw the flaming bush that was not consumed by fire he knew you were present. Then he heard your voice calling his name and he responded in awe and reverence. He answered your call on behalf of his people because he loved you to the core of his being. Although Moses doubted he could succeed, he held his faith high and was infused with grace. Your will and his became one and the Jewish people were freed from bondage.[1]

The burning bush is a living symbol that is embraced by Jewish people all over the world. It symbolizes the fact, that despite all the inhumane atrocities committed against them throughout the ages; they have never been consumed.[2] Your Divine Plan, Abba, is indeed ever present.

When one begins to realize that each of us is created with a soul that is empowered by your divine light, the magnitude of your love for us is unveiled. To become centered in you is to have the opportunity to create a personal living history that acknowledges all is from you and ultimately for you.[3] It is our love for you, Abba, that empowers us to claim our personhood. With you our Triune God, we have the opportunity to find meaning in our lives, and we are strengthened. All of us are called to meet the needs of our suffering humanity. Yet, the choice to do so is ours.

A Reading

> ... Just as the sun is fixed in the firmament of heaven and has power over the creatures of the Earth so that nothing can overcome them, so also believers who have their hearts and minds directed toward God cannot be forgotten by God.[4]

Psalm Response

Bless the Lord, O my soul;
all my being, bless his holy name!
Bless the Lord, O my soul;
and forget not all his benefits,
He pardons all your iniquities,
he heals all your ills.
He redeems your life from destruction,
he crowns you with kindness and compassion,
He fills your lifetime with good;
your youth is renewed like the eagle's.

*The Lord secures justice
and the rights of all the oppressed.
He has made known his ways to Moses,
and his deeds to the children of Israel.
Merciful and gracious is the Lord,
slow to anger and abounding in kindness.*

*The Lord has established his throne in heaven,
and his kingdom rules over all.
Bless the Lord, all you his angels,
you mighty in strength, who do his bidding,
obeying his spoken word!
Bless the Lord, all you hosts,
his ministers, who do God's will.
Bless the Lord, all his works,
everywhere in his domain.
Bless the Lord, O my soul!
Amen.*
        Psalm 103:1-8, 19-22

THE CHALLENGE

How have you allowed God to direct your life?

Have you ever thought God might be calling you to assist others? What have you done about it? Why not discuss it with your Parish Priest?

The Exodus

CLOCKWISE: *Moses is called to free the Israelites; The Passover of the Lord; The cloud by day and fire by night; The sea is split in two.*

SCRIPTURE

God ... said to Moses, "I am the Lord. As God the Almighty I appeared to Abraham, Isaac and Jacob, but my name Lord, I did not make known to them. I also established my covenant with them, to give them the land of Canaan, the land in which they were living as aliens. And now that I have heard the groaning of the Israelites whom the Egyptians are treating as slaves, I am mindful of my covenant. Therefore say to the Israelites: I am the Lord. I will free you from the forced labor of the Egyptians and will deliver you from their slavery, I will receive you by my outstretched arm and with mighty acts of judgment will make you as my own people, and you shall have me as your God. You will know that I, the Lord am your God. You will know that I, the Lord am your God when I free you from the labor of the Egyptians and bring you into the land, which I swore to give to Abraham, Isaac and Jacob. I will give it to you as your own possession.
    Exodus 6:2-8

The Lord said to Moses and Aaron in the land of Egypt, "This month shall stand at the head of your calendar. ... Tell the whole community of Israel: On the tenth of this month every one of your families must provide for itself a lamb. ... That same night they shall eat its roasted flesh with unleavened bread and bitter herbs. ... It is the Passover of the Lord. For on this same night I will go through Egypt, striking down every first-born of the land. ... But the blood will mark the houses where you are. Seeing the blood, I will pass over you; thus, when I strike the land of Egypt, no destructive blow will come upon you.
    Exodus 12:1-3, 8, 12, 13

At midnight the Lord slew every first born in the land of Egypt. ... During the night Pharaoh summoned Moses and Aaron and said, "Leave my people at once, you and the Israelites with you."
    Exodus 12:29,31

> *The Israelites set out from Rameses for Succoth, about six hundred thousand men on foot, not counting the children.*
> Exodus 12:37

> *The Lord preceded them, in the daytime by means of a column of cloud to show them the way, and at night by means of a column of fire to give them light.*
> Exodus 13:21

> *When it was reported to the king of Egypt that the people had fled, Pharaoh and his servants changed their minds. ... So Pharaoh made his chariots ready and mustered his soldiers. ... Pharaoh was already near when the Israelites ... saw that the Egyptians were on the march in pursuit of them. ... Then the Lord said to Moses, "Why are you crying out to me? Tell the Israelites to go forward. And you, lift up your staff and, with hand outstretched ... split the sea in two ... ." The Egyptians followed in pursuit ... right into the midst of the sea. Then the Lord told Moses "Stretch out your hand over the sea, that the water may flow back over the Egyptians ... ."*
> Exodus 14:5, 6, 10, 15, 23, 26

THOUGHTS

Abba

Your Passover was indeed a dark night. "A 'watch night' for the children of Israel."[1] From embittered slavery you led your chosen ones to freedom. It was you who enabled Moses to divide the Red Sea; brought them to dry land; sustained them with manna and then led them to the land of Israel. There on Mt. Sinai you gave them the Torah, the Law. A guide for personhood meant to provide us with a moral sense of all that is good. Because of original sin, humanity must learn the hidden power of choice that lies within us. You have always known we must learn for ourselves that, "the golden fruits of the free ... ripen not in the dark and dismal dungeon of an enslaved soul."[2]

A Reading

The Israelites witnessed marvels; you also will witness marvels greater and more splendid than those, which accompanied them on their departure from Egypt. You did not see Pharaoh drowned with his armies, but you have seen the devil with his weapons overcome by the waters of baptism. The Israelites passed through the sea; you have passed from death to life. They were delivered from the Egyptians; you have been delivered from the powers of darkness.

In those days Christ was present to the Israelites as he followed them, but he is present to us in a much deeper sense. The Lord was with them because of the favor he showed to Moses; now he is with us not simply because of your obedience. After Egypt they dwelt in desert places; after your departure you will dwell in heaven.

In those days Moses raised his hands to heaven and brought down Manna, the bread of angels; the new Moses raised his hands to heaven and gives us the food of eternal life. Moses struck the rock and brought forth streams of water; Christ touches his table, strikes the spiritual rock of the new covenant and draws forth the living water of the spirit. This rock is like a fountain in the midst of Christ's table, so that on all sides, the flocks may draw near to this living spring and refresh themselves in the waters of salvation.[3]

Psalm Response

I will bless the Lord at all times;
his praise shall be ever in my mouth.
Let my soul glory in the Lord;
the lowly will hear me and be glad.
Glorify the Lord with me,
let us together extol his name,

I sought the Lord and he answered
and delivered me from all my fears.
Look to him that you may be radiant with joy.
Taste and see how good the Lord is.
Amen.
    Psalm 34:2-6, 9

The Challenge

Think about a time that you or someone you knew lived in bondage. What freed them?

Think about the word freedom. How do you define freedom now? How does it differ from your previous concept?

The Ten Commandments

Scripture

Then God delivered all these commandments: "I the Lord am your God, who brought you out of the land of Egypt, that place of slavery. You shall not have other gods beside me. You shall not take the name of the Lord your God, in vain. Remember to keep the Sabbath day. Honor your father and your mother. ... You shall not kill. You shall not commit adultery. You shall not steal. You shall not bear false witness against your neighbor. You shall not covet your neighbors' house. You shall not covet your neighbor's wife."
        Exodus 20:1-3, 7, 8, 12-17

When the Pharisees heard that he had silenced the Sadducees, they gathered together and one of them (a scholar of the law) tested him by asking, "Teacher, which commandment in the law is the greatest?" He said to him, "You shall love the Lord, your God, with all your heart, with all your soul, and with all your mind. This is the greatest and the first commandment. The second is like it: You shall love your neighbor as yourself. The whole law and the prophets depend on these two commandments."
        Matthew 22:34-40

Thoughts

Abba

Conferred by You, our Creator, The Ten Commandments are of your Divine Will and as such carry both a blessing and a warning. They are the foundation of our Judeo-Christian heritage. They are the standard of moral law. Blessed, with free will, each of us has the ability to choose how we will live out our lives. The question is: Will we misuse your gift, or will we center you in our lives and collaborate with your divine will? Will we choose to live responsibly, in order to live out our personhood with dignity?

Only the power of sin can separate us from your beloved son. Yet, when we allow ourselves to hear that voice in the desert ... calling each of us to repent; to cleanse ourselves in righteousness, we have the ability to experience your blessing. It is within the New Covenant, codified in love, that we sinners learn; we are never beyond your grace. We are never beyond your everlasting mercy.

A Reading

God's word does not change. The Ten Commandments given to Moses are perfected, but also reconfirmed by Jesus when he declared "... *not an iota, not a dot will pass from the law until all is accomplished*" (Matt 5:18). Jesus is teaching us to observe the law with a new spirit of love and interiority, but the law still remains in its essential elements an expression of the immutable will of God. For this reason it is loving faithfulness to the law that will decide our eternal fate. *Whoever relaxes one of the least of these commandments ... shall be called least in the kingdom of heaven: but he who does them ... shall be called great. We are great, not when we free ourselves from God, but when we adhere to the will of God, we partake of his holiness, his goodness and his wisdom. The law of God said Moses to Israel, is your wisdom and your understanding* (Deut 4:6).[1]

Psalm Response

The law of the Lord is perfect,
refreshing the soul;
The decree of the Lord is trustworthy,
giving wisdom to the simple.
The precepts of the Lord are right,
rejoicing the heart;
The command of the Lord is clear,
enlightening the eye;
The fear of the Lord is pure,
enduring forever.
The ordinances of the Lord are true, all of them just;
They are more precious than gold,
than a heap of purest gold;
Sweeter also than syrup
or honey from the comb.

Though your servant is careful of them,
very diligent in keeping them,
Yet who can detect failings?
Cleanse me from my unknown faults!
From wanton sin especially,
restrain your servant;
let it not rule over me.
Then shall I be blameless and innocent of serious sin.
Let the words of my mouth and the thought of my heart
find favor beside you,
O Lord, my rock and my redeemer.
Amen.
    Psalm 19 B 8-15

The Challenge

When you use the Ten Commandments as your moral standard, how does it help you make a decision?

The Ratification of the Covenant

Scripture

When Moses came to the people and related all the words and ordinances of the Lord, they all answered with one voice: "We will do everything that the Lord has told us." Moses then wrote down all the words of the Lord and, rising early the next day, he erected at the floor of the mountain an altar and twelve pillars for the twelve tribes of Israel. Then having sent certain young men of the Israelites to offer holocausts and sacrifice young bulls as peace offerings to the Lord, Moses took half of the blood and put it in large bowls; the other half he splashed on the altar. Taking the book of the covenant, he read it aloud to the people, who answered, "All that the Lord has said, we will heed and do." Then he took the blood and sprinkled it on the people, saying, "This is the blood of the covenant which the Lord has made with you in accordance with all these words of his."
    Exodus 24:3-8

Thoughts

Abba

You always meant to lead your Chosen Ones, the Israelites to life: to live in communion with you. Before the beginning of time, you planned a kingdom of holy people. A nation centered in you; appreciating the wonder of the universe. You hoped each would become a steward of the land and would live harmoniously together in commitment to your covenant. For them you laid a foundation for living life and within its fold was your promise. It was a "covenant of love," a transcendent act circumscribed in the sacredness of blood; the seat of life and a sacred conduit for atonement.[1,2,3] Despite the fact that in their humanness your chosen ones failed to meet their obligations, you continued to pursue them through the voices of your prophets. You understood human weakness and you refused to give up. So it was that you sent your only son Jesus to dwell ... *among us and we saw his glory, the glory as of the Father's only Son full of grace and truth* (John 1:14). The promised Messiah walked with us, his mission; to teach us how to live out our lives centered in love and truth. From the beginning, Abba, you knew if we were to live out our obligation to you, Jesus had to become the

Sacrificial Lamb, the never-ending wellspring of your divine love and our Redeemer. With His death, the Old Covenant was fulfilled. *It was not through the law that the promise was made to Abraham and his descendents that he would inherit the world, but through the righteousness that comes from faith* (Rom 4: 13)[4]

Your Son died for all of us because of our ... *transgressions and was raised for our justification* (Rom 4:25). ... *Since we have been justified by faith we have peace with (you, Abba) through our Lord, Jesus Christ through whom we have gained access (by faith) to this grace* ... (Rom 5:1). It was Jesus who atoned for our sins and gave us life anew. It was in His dying that Jesus visibly expressed His total love for both you, Abba, and for all of us. It is that response that resounds in our hearts forever and ever. [5]

A Reading

Under the Old Law, when God told His people that they must love their neighbor as themselves, it was before He had come upon earth Himself; knowing how much man loved him, it was the best He could ask. But when Jesus gives His Apostles a New Commandment (John 13:34), His own Commandment (John 15:12), He asks them to love another, not only as they love themselves, but as He Himself loves them, and will love them even unto the consummation of the world!

Yet I know, my Jesus, that You never command the impossible. You know better than I how frail and imperfect I am, You know perfectly well that I can never hope to love my Sisters as You love them unless You Yourself love them in me.

It is only because You are willing to do this that You have given us a New Commandment, and I love it because it is my assurance of Your desire to love in me all those whom You command me to love.[6]

The Book of Ruth

CLOCKWISE: *The crossroads; Naomi and Ruth return to Bethlehem; Ruth meets Boaz; Ruth presents herself; Boaz and the Elders; Boaz marries Ruth; Obed is born and placed in the arms of Naomi.*

Psalm Response

O Lord, our Lord
how glorious is your name over all the earth!
You have exalted your majesty
above the heavens,
Out of the mouths of babes and sucklings
you have fashioned praise because of your foes
to silence the hostile and the vengeful
When I behold your heavens, the work of your fingers,
the moon and the stars which you
set in place-
What is man that you should be
mindful of him,
or the son of man that you should care for him?

You have made him little less that the angels
and crowned him with glory and honor
You have given him rule over the
works of your hands
Putting all things under his feet:
All sheep and oxen,
yes and the beasts of the field
The birds of the air, the fishes of the sea
and whatever swims the paths of the sea
O Lord, our Lord
how glorious is your name over all the earth.
Amen.
    Psalm 8:2-10

The Challenge

How obedient are we to the Father's will? What challenges has God placed before us?

What does being a member of the new covenant mean to you?

SCRIPTURE

"Ruth said, do not ask me to abandon or forsake you! For wherever you go I will go, wherever you lodge I will lodge, your people shall be my people and your God my God."
    Ruth 1:16

THOUGHTS

Abba

Such simple words, yet so exquisite to the ear; they have become immortalized. They are words that reflect a decision made at a crossroad in life. They are words spoken during ancient times by Ruth, a Moabite who converted to Judaism. They are the record of a young woman totally immersed in your endless pool of love; a soul that had died to self and was filled with life-giving generosity. Ruth was indeed anchored within the fold of your covenant of love.

None of us is just a traveler within our own story. If we look back to decisions made at crossroads during our own lifetime, we will find evidence that marks our character. These traits carry us into the present. They are our personal imprints that reflect both our strengths and our weaknesses. Though Ruth's husband died, she recognized in her loss that loving connections enrich life. For Ruth, her present family was her mother-in-law. Ruth chose to be loyal, to be faithful, to be family and, as a result, was able to affirm life not only for her mother-in-law, but as well for herself. Naomi was in the throes of despair. She was suffering the loss of her husband, as well, and the loss of her two sons. Yet we learn Naomi responded to her community of friends and began to teach Ruth the traditions of living life in a covenant community. Unselfishly, she also understood Ruth needed to be married. Both were thoughtful of the other and practiced generosity because they loved you and had centered their lives in the 'torah'. The capacity for good and evil exists in all of us. It is during times of despair that one struggles with the inevitability of "what is." The question is where one draws strength. Both drew strength from you, Abba.

Crossroads met during one's life are sacred moments in time. They are life-defining, and we come to each, free to choose our own path. The hand of Divine Providence is rarely known, only realized. Who would believe in that little community of covenant believers, that Ruth a convert, would marry Naomi's cousin, Boaz; have a child who would one day have a son named Jesse, who would become the father of King David and an ancestor of the living Messiah, Jesus, your Son? Life is indeed all blessing and we must strive to remember just that!

A Reading

Thoughtfulness is the beginning of great sanctity. If you learn this art of being thoughtful, you will become more and more Christ like, for his heart was meek and he always thought of the needs of others.[1]

Psalm Response

To you we owe our hymns of praise,
O God, in Zion;
To you must vows be fulfilled,
you who hear prayers
To you all flesh must come ...
Happy the man you choose, and bring
to dwell in your court.
Amen.
      Psalm 65:1-3, 5

The Challenge

Look back to a decision you made at a crossroad in your life. How did it mark your character?

What lessons did you learn that are now anchors of your faith?

Solomon's Judgment

Scripture

... Two harlots came to the King and stood before him. One woman said, ... "By your leave my Lord, this woman and I live in the same house and I gave birth in the house while she was present. On the third day, after I gave birth, this woman also gave birth. We were alone in the house; there was no one there but us two. This woman's son died during the night: she smothered him by lying on him. Later that night she got up and took my son from my side, as I, your handmaid was sleeping. Then she laid him in her bosom after she laid the dead child in my bosom. I rose in the morning to nurse my child and I found him dead. But when I examined him in the morning light, I saw it was not the son whom I had borne."

The other woman answered, "It is not so. The living one is my son, the dead one is yours." But the first kept saying "No, the dead one is your child, the living one is mine!" Thus they argued before the King. ... Then the King said, "One woman claims, this, the living one is my child and the dead one is yours. The other answered, 'No, the dead one is your child; the living one is mine.'" The King continued, "Get me a sword" When they brought the sword before him he said, "Cut the living child in two and give half to one woman and half to the other. The woman whose son it was, in the anguish she felt for it said to the King, "Please my Lord, give her living child—please do not kill it!" The other said, "It shall be neither mine nor yours. Divide it!" The King then answered, "Give the first one the living child! By no means kill it, for she is the mother." When all Israel heard the judgment the King had given, they were in awe of him, because they saw that the King had in him the wisdom for giving judgment."
    1 Kings 3:16-29

Thoughts

Beloved Jesus

More times than not, we tend to succumb to our selfishness. Yet, if one truly loves another, acts of selflessness will be required. These are the moments in time that determine whether or not one is truly capable of loving unconditionally.

Selfless deeds stem from a soul imbued with your divine light. Loving you softens those crusty layers of self-love until the heart hears it own authentic voice calling for transparency. In that moment, the soul is freed of its need to protect itself and is able to risk loving unconditionally. The soul has learned it no longer needs to protect itself. It knows it is infused with your love.

A Reading

> Eternal Trinity ... you are a fire ever burning and never consumed, which itself consumes all the selfish love that fills my being. Yes, you are a fire that takes away the coldness, illuminates the mind with its light and causes me to know your truths. And I know that you are beauty and wisdom itself. The food of Angels you give yourself to man in the fire of your love.[1]

Psalm Response

> *I love the Lord because he has heard my voice in supplication*
> *Because he has inclined his ear to me the day I called*
> *The cords of death encompassed me;*
> *the snares of the nether world sized upon me;*
> *I fell into distress and sorrow*
> *And I called upon the name of the Lord*
> *"O Lord, save my life!"*

Gracious is the Lord and just;
yes our God is merciful.
The Lord keeps the little ones;
I was brought low and he saved me.
Return O my soul, to your tranquility
for the Lord has been good to you
For he has freed my soul from death,
my eyes from tears, my feet from stumbling
I shall walk before the Lord in the lands of the living.
Amen.
    Psalm 116:1-9

CHALLENGE

Think about those times when you were selfless. Thank God for those moments!

Out of the Whirlwind

Scripture

One day, when the sons of God came to present themselves before the Lord, Satan also came among them. And the Lord said to Satan, "whence do you come?" Then Satan answered the Lord and said, "From roaming the earth and patrolling it." And the Lord said to Satan, "Have you noticed my servant Job, and that there is no one on earth like him, blameless and upright, fearing God and avoiding evil?" But Satan answered the Lord and said, "Is it for not that Job is God-fearing? Have you not surrounded him and his family and all that he has within your protection? You have blessed the work of his hands, and his livestock are spread over the land. But now put forth your hand and touch everything he has, and surely he will blaspheme you to your face." And the Lord said to Satan, "Behold, all that he has is in your power; only do not lay a hand upon his person." So Satan went forth from the presence of the Lord.
    Job 1:6-13

Thoughts

Abba

It is in the darkness of grief that one learns everything is of You. Life altering experiences teach us the outer limits of our human condition and we are forever humbled. We become Job and we begin to realize *there is no authority except from God* (Rom 13-1). What we seek is to know You, for without knowing You, life is without meaning.[1] With contrition on our lips and repentance in our heart, we learn your mercy is always present. In the outpouring of your light we also learn all is grace.

Life-altering experiences are profoundly painful and our need for the sacred overrides all other needs. When one enters the realm of emptiness, we are forced to acknowledge that we are simply creatures. We have reached the limit of our finite self and only the one, who is "infinite," can comfort us. It is as if we must become enjoined in our suffering if we are to begin to experience your compassion within the walls of our broken self. The Spirit groans. Your Son is calling us to be one with Him. And as that happens, on that life-bearing cross, we begin to understand with a certain sense of knowing that "every acceptance of suffering, is an acceptance of what exists."[2]

The story of Job is not about why we suffer. Rather, it is about our need to center You, our Triune God, in our universe. It is a story about being justified in faith. Job was a descendant of Abraham. He was a just man who *did not weaken in faith. ... He did not doubt God's promises in unbelief. ... He was empowered by faith and gave glory to God* (Rom 19:20). Job learned that *affliction produces endurance, and endurance proven character, and proven character hope, and hope does not disappoint, because the love of God* was in his heart (Rom 5:3-5). Job simply needed to have an "intimate and personal relationship with You, (Abba,) that was not based on the mere exchange of gifts or services, but on a communion of love."[3]

A Reading

Certainly, like everybody, I have known anger and I have raised my voice in protest. I do not regret it. But over the years, I have come to understand the double-edged nature of the questioning that modern man endures: even as I have the right to ask the Judge of all men, "why did you allow Auschwitz to happen?" So has He the right to ask us, "Why have you made a mess of my creation? By what right have you cut down the trees of life and made them altars to death?" And all of a sudden you think of God in his heavenly and luminous loneliness, and you feel like weeping. For Him and over Him. And you weep so much that He too—so many Talmudic traditions—He too begins to weep, until your tears and His come together and merge like two melancholy solitudes, thirsting for fulfillment.[4]

Psalm Response

Only in God be at rest, my soul,
for from him comes my hope.
He only is my rock and my salvation

my stronghold; I shall not be disturbed.
With God is my safety and my glory,
he is the rock of my strength; my
refuge is in God.
Trust in him at all times. O my people!
Pour out your hearts before him
God is our refuge
Amen.
      Psalm 62: 6-9

THE CHALLENGE

How has a life-altering experience brought you or someone you know closer to God?

The Story of Tobit

CLOCKWISE: *Tobit buries the dead; Tobit is blinded at the wall; Sarah's plight; a Father's instruction; Tobiah and the Angel Raphael; by the Tigris river; the journey to the house of Raguel; the marriage of Tobiah and Sarah; expulsion of the demon; Tobits's sight is restored; Raphael's identity is made known.*

Scripture

The Book of Tobit

Thoughts

Abba

Hidden within this book of ancient folklore, lies a remarkable tale that is filled with lessons to learn from our ancestors: Their commitment to your covenant and their desire to pass on to their children the need to adhere to your law (Tob 4:13-19). Most of all we learn you always hear the prayers of the poor in spirit. It was You who sent the angel Raphael in the form of a stranger to heal them (Tob 3:12; 12:2). In its sheer simplicity, The Book of Tobit imparts the absolute wonder of You, Abba, in all your majesty.

Yet, there is one additional lesson to learn. It is about learning to accept the fact that we can never change the past, but we can accept its challenge. For some like Sarah, the heroine, her past was a place of fearsome shadows. Thrown into despair, she turned to You, Abba, in prayer and found that You were her true center. Through prayer, she surrendered to divine providence and as she did so began to experience your luminous peace. Within the mind's ear, one can imagine almost hearing you say to her, *"I have heard your prayer and seen your tears"* (2 Kgs 20:8). So it is in real time the self learns it neither needs to shut down, nor try to control life; rather, it can trust in you with faith. Only then is the self free to accept the present and whatever the future may hold. It has learned for itself the importance of surrendering to all that is unknown. The soul has learned to accept with humility the reality that whatever is … is. Whatever will be … is. For all that exists is … as it is.

Although we may never understand why certain things happen, if we look back, we will remember those particular times as having a tremendous impact upon our lives. Spend a little more time with this sacred story and recall the miracle of the Angel Raphael. He appeared in the person of a 'special one', who gave aide to those who were vulnerable. Indeed, Abba, you always hear the prayers of the poor in spirit![1]

A Reading

If the virtue of humility teaches us not to rely on ourselves alone, the virtue of faith teaches us to trust in God. In fact, the very word faith (fides) connotes confidence or trust. Hence, Saint James advises us to *petition the Lord with faith, never doubting because the doubter cannot expect to receive anything from the Lord* (Jas 1:6). And Jesus has told us: *"You will receive all that you ask for, provided you have faith"* (Matt 21:22).

But now you may ask how you can have that kind of faith and confidence when you have done so little for God. The answer is that the basis for faith and confidence is not what you have done for God, but the goodness and mercy of God and the merits of the Passion and death of Jesus Christ. Remember God is infinite and so also is his mercy. Therefore, when you approach God with your petitions, do not be timid or afraid. He is our Father and we are his children; in asking him with childlike confidence to grant us what we need we are giving glory to God.[2]

Psalm Response

You who dwell in the shelter of the Most High
who abide in the shadow of the Almighty.
Say to the Lord, "My refuge and my fortress
my God in whom I trust"
For he will rescue you from the snare of the fowler,
from the destroying pestilence.
With his pinions he will cover you,
and under his wings you shall take refuge;
his faithfulness is a buckler and a shield,
You shall not fear the terror of the night
nor the arrow that flies by day;
Not the pestilence that roams in the darkness
nor the devastating plague at noon.
Because you have the Lord for your refuge;

You have made the Most High your stronghold.
... to his angels he has given command about you,
that they guard you all your ways
Upon their hands they shall bear you up.
Amen.
   Psalm 91:1-6, 9-12

THE CHALLENGE

Think about those times in your life when you have been most vulnerable. How did you handle those moments in time?

If you are now experiencing a difficult time or are stuck in a memory that keeps you from moving on, why not talk to God about it?

Do you believe in Angels? Has the Angel Raphael ever entered your life? Perhaps you will share that moment with someone who needs to hear your story.

The Book of Esther

CLOCKWISE: *Mordecai refuses to bow before Haman; The decree of Ahasuerus was cast; Mordecai talks to Esther; Esther covers herself with ashes; Esther calls upon the king on behalf of her people; Haman is destroyed; Esther is crowned Queen.*

SCRIPTURE

"All the King's servants who were at the royal gate would kneel and bow down to Haman, for that is what the king had ordered in his regard. Mordecai, however, would not kneel and bow down. The king's servants who were at the royal gate said to Mordecai "Why do you disobey the king's order?" When they had reminded him day after day and he would not listen to them, they informed Haman, to see whether Mordecai's explanation was acceptable, since he had told them he was a Jew. When Haman observed that Mordecai would not kneel and bow down to him, he was filled with anger. Moreover, he thought it was not enough to lay hands on Mordecai alone. Since they had told Haman of Mordecai's nationality, he sought to destroy all the Jews, Mordecai's people, throughout the realm of King Ahasuerus. In the first month, Nisan, in the twelfth year of King Ahasuerus, the pur or lot, was cast in Haman's presence to determine the day and month for the destruction of Mordecai's people. Then Haman said to King Ahasuerus: "Dispersed among the nations throughout the provinces of your kingdom, there are a certain people living apart, with laws differing from those of every other people. They do not obey the laws of the king and so it is not proper for the king to tolerate them. If it pleases the king, let a decree be issued to destroy them ... and I will deliver to the procurators ten thousand silver talents for deposit in the royal treasury." The King took the signet ring from his hand and gave it to Haman, son of Hammedatha the Agagite, the enemy of the Jews. "The silver you may keep," the king said to Haman, "but as for this people, do with them whatever you please." Letters were sent by couriers to all the royal provinces, that all the Jews young and old, including women and children, should be killed, destroyed, wiped out in one day, the thirteenth day of the twelfth month, Adar, and that their goods should be seized as spoil.

Esther 3:2-11, 13

Thoughts

Abba

In the sacred stories of the past, there are many lessons to be learned. One example is the decree of Ahasuerus in the Book of Esther. It stands as a reminder of the chilling effects of totalitarian regimes.[1] Indelibly preserved for time everlasting is its haunting imprint of discrimination; a dark and evil shadow that breeds intolerance until its malevolent cause degenerates into a Haman, a Hitler, or a killing field, a Bosnia, a Rwanda, or the gassing of the Kurds. The Book of Esther is the story of a young Jewish woman who had to learn how to face such an ordeal on behalf of her people with courage and conviction. It is the story of her transformation into a woman of valor. It is also a story about the liberation of the Jewish people form the throes of a pogrom.[2]

Queen Esther was orphaned as a child and was brought up by her Uncle Mordecai. She was very beautiful and when there was an opportunity to become the King's consort, her uncle fearing she would be discriminated against, advised her to hide her Jewish identity. After Esther advanced to the King's court, her Uncle Mordecai enraged the tyrant Haman. Because of religious conviction, he refused to kneel before him. In turn, Haman became so angry that he provoked the King to issue the Decree of Ahasuerus, which threatened Mordecai and all the Jewish people of the region with extinction.

Mordecai called upon Esther to save them. To do so meant she would have to develop a sense of consciousness, an inner strength that was based upon truth, understanding and compassion. Queen Esther needed to become authentic. Understandably she was frightened. She knew she would be placing herself in jeopardy and that her actions could result in death. Although her Uncle comprehended her fear, he also realized if Esther was to respond to the needs of their people, he would have to challenge her to look deep within herself. So he replied. *"Do not imagine that because you are in the king's palace, you alone of all the Jews will escape. Even if you now remain silent, relief and deliverance will come to the Jews from another source; but you and your father's house will perish. Who knows but that it was for a time like this that you obtained the royal dignity?"* (Esth 4:12). These words, Abba, echo your call that we remember; what is providential, is anchored in hope and duty.

It was you, Abba, who called Esther. You called her on behalf of your chosen people to collaborate with your will. With a humbled heart Esther repented, calling upon your mercy. Covering herself with ashes she symbolically noted the reality of her personhood, her sinfulness and that all returns to dust.[3] Then she called for the support of the Jewish community to join with her in a fast and as reported in scripture, prayed for three days. On the third day Esther emerged with a new sense of consciousness. She was filled with courage and fortitude. Queen Esther was transformed into a woman of valor and her people were saved. With you, Abba, fear is conquered. With prayer, truth is found and with it one's moral integrity.

So you see, Abba, it is in the stories of old that we have the opportunity to find you and learn lessons in living!

A Reading

> The life of each one of us is, as it were, woven of those two threads: the thread of inward development through which our ideas and affections and our human and mystical attitudes are gradually formed; and the thread of outward success by which we always find ourselves at the exact point at which the totality of the forces of the universe converge to produce upon us the effect which God desires.
>
> O God, that at all times you may find me as You desire me and where You would have me be, that you may lay hold on me fully, both by the Within and the Without of myself. Grant that I may never break this double thread of my life.[4]

Psalm Response

Sin speaks to the wicked man in his heart;
there is no dread of God before his eyes.
For he beguiles himself with the thought
that his guilt will not be found out or hated.

The words of his mouth are empty and false;
he has ceased to understand how to do good.
He plans wickedness in his bed;
he sets out on a way that is not good,
with no repugnance for evil.

O Lord, your kindness reaches to heaven;
your faithfulness, to the clouds.
Your justice is like the mountains of God:
your judgments, like the mighty deep;
man and beast you save O Lord.

How precious is your kindness, O God!
The children of men take refuge
in the shadow of your wings
They have their fill of the prime gifts of your house:
from your delightful stream you give them drink.
For with you is the fountain of life,
and in your light we see light.
Amen.
    Psalm 36:1-10

THE CHALLENGE

Think about the reading by Pierre Teilhard de Chardin. How do you perceive the two threads that are being woven within your life?

Do you see how God has affected your life?

Part Two:
From the New Testament

"Beloved, let us love one another, because love is of God; everyone who loves is begotten by God and knows God. Whoever is without love does not know God, for God is Love."
 1 John 4:7-8

Mary, the Mother of God

Scripture

In the sixth month, the angel Gabriel was sent from God to a town of Galilee, called Nazareth, to a Virgin betrothed to a man named Joseph of the house of David, and the Virgin's name was Mary. And coming to her, he said, "Hail, favored one! The Lord is with you." But she was greatly troubled at what was said and pondered what sort of greeting this might be. Then the angel said to her, "Do not be afraid, Mary, for you have found favor with God. Behold you will conceive in your womb and bear a son, and you shall name him Jesus. He will be great and will be called Son of the Most High, and the Lord God will give him the throne of David, his father, and he will rule over the house of Jacob forever, and of his kingdom there will be no end." But Mary said to the Angel, "How can this be, since I have no relations with a man?" And the Angel said to her in reply, "The holy Spirit will come upon you, and the power of the Most High will overshadow you. Therefore, the child to be born will be called holy, the Son of God."
    Luke 1:26-35

Thoughts

Abba

By virtue of expressed grace, Mary, a daughter of Abraham was conceived without fault. In unparalleled humility and faith-filled reverence, she adhered to your will. Mary understood you are the Author of all that is. And, in one incomprehensible moment, our world was forever changed. Her yes ... her gift to humanity; your son ... our Lord ... Jesus Christ.

A Reading

Abraham's faith stands at the beginning of the Old Covenant, so Mary's faith at the Annunciation opens the New Covenant. Mary's faith like Abraham means trust in

God and obedience, even when one walks in darkness. It means letting go of oneself, freeing oneself, surrendering oneself in view of the truth of God.[1]

Psalm Response

Sing to the Lord a new song;
sing to the Lord, all you lands.
Sing to the Lord: bless his name;
announce his salvation, day after day.
Tell his glory among nations
among all peoples, his wondrous deeds.
For great is the Lord and highly to be praised
awesome is he, beyond all gods.
For all the gods of the nations are
things of naught,
but the Lord made the heavens,
Splendor and majesty go before him;
praise and grandeur are in his sanctuary.

Give to the Lord, you families of nations
give to the Lord glory and praise;
give to the Lord the glory due his name.
Bring gifts and enter his courts;
worship the Lord in holy attire.
Tremble before him, all the earth,
say among the nations; The Lord is king
He has made the world firm, not to be moved;
he governs the people with equity.

Let the heavens be glad and the earth rejoice;
let the sea and what fills it resound;
let the plains be joyful and all that is in them.
Then shall all the trees of the forest exalt
before the Lord, for he comes;
for he comes to rule the earth
He shall rule the world with justice
and the peoples with his constancy.
Amen
  Psalm 96

The Challenge

How have you centered Mary, the Mother of God in your life?

The Visitation

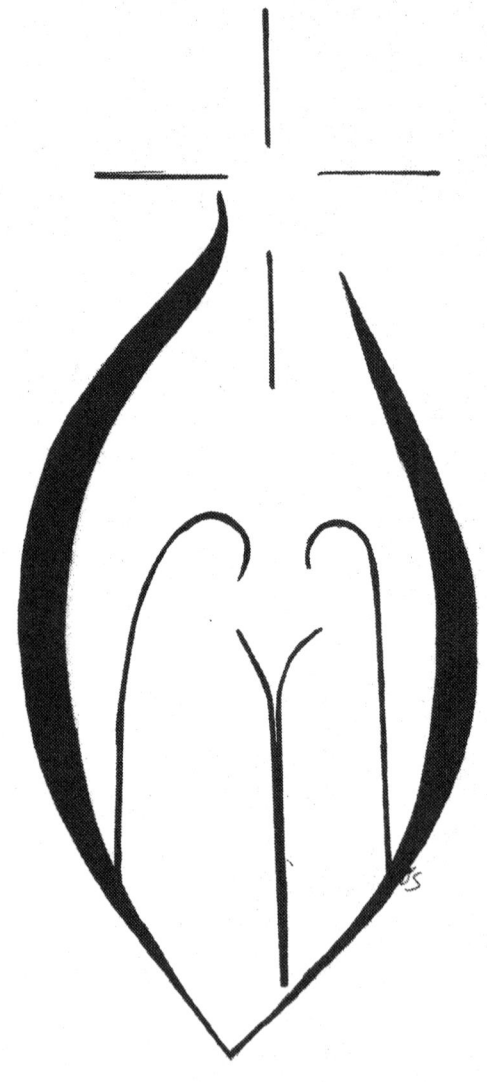

SCRIPTURE

During those days Mary set out and traveled to the hill country in haste to a town of Judah, where she entered the house of Zechariah and greeted Elizabeth. When Elizabeth heard Mary's greeting the infant leaped in her womb, and Elizabeth, filled with the holy Spirit cried out in a loud voice and said, "Most blessed are you among women and blessed is the fruit of your womb. And how does this happen to me? That the mother of my Lord should come to me? For at the moment the sound of your greeting reached my ears, the infant in my womb leaped for joy. Blessed are you who believed that what was spoken to you by the Lord would be fulfilled."
   Luke 1:39-45

THOUGHTS

Abba

To enter into the center of your love is to be enfolded within the mystery of faith; an everlasting moment that ushers in an awakening to your Divine Plan. You grace us with your love until the very essence of one's soul is seeded and begins to sprout acts of kindness preceded by a most humbled heart. ... *The light of your countenance shines upon us!* (Ps 4:7). It was your salvific plan that gifted both Mary and her older cousin, Elizabeth, with the miracle of life. "Mary and Elizabeth were chosen as vital instruments in the work of salvation."[1] We too, are called to believe no matter the cost: To love much, to trust and pray into the silence with hope.[2]

Mary believed and her cousin Elizabeth affirmed her belief. "*How does this happen to me, the mother of my Lord should come to me ... for at the sound of your greeting the infant in my womb leaped for joy. Blessed are you who believed ... .*" (Luke 1:42-45). With these words uttered by Elizabeth, your Divine Plan for our world was cast forever.

The question is, do we believe and ... have we remembered ... to thank you?

A Reading

God is a giver of gifts. For Mary and Elizabeth that was the gift of new life. For each of us the gift of time, the gift of freedom and opportunity, the gift of grace.

Reception of gifts is not enough. We must give thanks: we must become an enchanted people. Thankfulness comes in two forms: words of gratitude and gifts shared joyfully and with charity. A test will always be the ability to give thanks for both good and difficult experiences. Beneath thankfulness lies faith. We believe, as Mary and Elizabeth that an eternal light illumines all creation and that even death cannot extinguish the flame. Here is a deep gratitude that leads to peace.[3]

Psalm Response

My soul, gives thanks to the Lord
all my being, bless His holy name.
My soul, gives thanks to the Lord
and never forgets all his blessings.

It is he who forgives all your guilt
who heals every one of your ills
who redeems your life from the grave,
who crowns you with love and compassion
who fills you life with good things,
renewing your youth like eagle's.

The Lord does deeds of justice
gives judgment for all who are oppressed.
He made known his ways to Moses
and his deeds to Israel's sons.

The Lord is compassion and love,
slow to anger and rich in mercy.
His wrath will come to an end;

he will not be angry for ever.
He does not treat us according to our sins
nor repay us according to our faults
For as the heavens are high about the earth
so strong is his love for those who fear Him
Amen.
      Psalm 103[4]

THE CHALLENGE

List all the gifts you have received from God. Have you thanked Him?

Think about a person in your life who affirms the essence of your being. Thank God for that person's presence in your life.

The Presentation of Our Lord in the Temple

Scripture

When the days were completed for their purification according to the law of Moses, they took him up to Jerusalem to present him to the Lord, just as it is written in the law of the Lord, "Every male that opens the womb shall be consecrated to the Lord," and to offer the sacrifice of "a pair of turtledoves or two young pigeons," in accordance with the dictate in the law of the Lord.

Now there was a man in Jerusalem whose name was Simeon. This man was righteous and devout, awaiting the consolation of Israel and the holy Spirit was upon him. It had been revealed to him by the Holy Spirit that he should not see death before he had seen the Messiah of the Lord. He came in the Spirit into the temple; and when the parents brought in the child Jesus to perform the custom of the law in regard to him he took him into his arms and blessed God saying:

"Now Master, you may let your servant go
in peace, according to your word,
for my eyes have seen your salvation,
which you prepared in sight of all the peoples.
a light for revelation to the Gentiles,
and glory to your people Israel."

The child's father and mother were amazed at what was said about him; and Simeon blessed them and said to Mary his mother, "Behold, this child is destined for the fall and rise of many in Israel, and to be a sign that will be contradicted (and you yourself a sword will pierce) so that the thoughts of many hearts may be revealed."

There was also a prophetess, Anna, the daughter of Phanuel, of the tribe of Asher. She was advanced in years, having lived seven years with her husband after her marriage, and then as a widow until she was eighty-four. She never left the temple, but worshipped night and day with fasting and prayer. And coming forward at that very time, she gave thanks to God and spoke about the child to all who were awaiting the redemption of Jerusalem.
    Luke 2:22-39

Thoughts

Beloved Jesus

It is not difficult to imagine that wondrous day of long ago when you were but an infant. With hearts beating as one, your Holy Family brought you to the Temple. It was your first visit to your Father's house. It was the day of your presentation and for your Mother a day of purification. It was a day prescribed by the Law of Moses. Because your family was devout and very poor: *their sacrifice and sin offering, a pair of turtledoves* (Lev 12:1-8). Though we know now there was never a need for purification or a sin offering, your parents followed precisely the Torah. They were people of the covenant.[1]

There in the Temple, Simeon, who was a very pious man, recognized you in the light of your glory. The holy Spirit was upon him. He knew the Messiah had arrived. He knew he was holding the hope of the world. He knew you had arrived into your sanctuary for our redemption and as he blessed you he prophesied that *a sword* would *pierce* your mother's heart *so that the thoughts of many hearts may be revealed* (Luke 2:35). Simeon knew your mother would become a comfort and guiding light for those in need forever and ever. But, Simeon wasn't the only one to recognize you that day. The prophetess Anna upon seeing you offered thanks to your Father in heaven. There you were, on that day of long ago in the Temple in Jerusalem: the living fulfillment of the dream, the light of Truth—a wondrous mystery! And from a place somewhere deep inside, we now understand, to be in communion with you is to walk in self-awareness and in love. How blessed we are to have the opportunity to prepare ourselves for that time when we will be presented to you in that place of everlasting life.

A Reading

> We all run to you, O Christ, we who sincerely and profoundly adore your mystery: we set out towards you, full of joy ... carrying lighted candles, as a symbol of your divine splendor.

Thanks to you, all creation is radiant; in truth it is inundated by an eternal light, which dissipates the shadows of evil. But let these lighted candles be especially the symbol of the eternal splendor with which we wish to prepare ourselves for our meeting with you, O Christ. Indeed just as your Mother, the most pure Virgin, carried in her arms you who are the true light, and showed you to all who find themselves in darkness, so may we also, hold in our hands this light that is visible to all, and who are illuminated by its shining, hasten to go to meet you, who are the true light … .

The light that enlightens every man who comes into the world has come. … All together we come to you, O Christ, to let ourselves be clothed with your splendor and, together with the old man Simeon, to welcome you, O eternal living light. With him we exult with you and sing a hymn of thanksgiving to God, Father of light, who sent us the true light to lead us out of darkness and to make us luminous.[2]

Psalm Response

The Lord is my light and my salvation:
whom should I fear?
The Lord is my life's refuge;
of whom should I be afraid?

One thing I ask of the Lord;
This I seek:
To dwell in the house of the Lord all the days of my life,
That I may gaze on the loveliness
of the Lord
and contemplate his temple.
For he will hide me in his abode
in the days of trouble;
He will conceal me in the shelter of his tent.
he will set me high upon a rock.
Even now my head is held high
above my enemies on every side.

*And I will offer in his tent
sacrifices with shouts of gladness;
I will sing and chant praise to the Lord.
Amen.*
        Psalm 27:1, 4-6

THE CHALLENGE

What is the significance of the presentation of Jesus in the Temple? What meaning does it have for you?

The Holy Family

Scripture

"I am the true vine and my father is the vine grower, I am the vine, you are the branches. Whoever remains in me and I in him will bear much fruit, because without me you can do nothing."
      John 15:1, 5

Thoughts

Beloved Jesus

You entreat us to enter into the fold of your Holy Family to look to them for inspiration and direction. Their union fills us with seeds for living. In shared belief, Mary and Joseph claimed the Father's blessing. Holding you close in trusting faith and obedience, they cast together a new reality.

You are our lifeline; a vine of boundless love and mercy and we your loving creatures are your branches. Family means living out your blessing. It means being mindful of our covenant obligations. Just as the Father *prepared the land, drenching its furrows, breaking up it clods, softening it with showers, blessing its yield* (Ps 65:11), so too are we called to sow seeds that live out our faith.

Family is also about sowing dreams. It is about loving with joy and a sense of selflessness that holds personhood and dignity synonymous. Family is about instilling and preserving traditions. It is about respect and learning to listen and honor difference. It is about holding to boundaries; yet becoming a natural haven for mutual help by and for each member including those of the preceding generation.

Yet, the reality is, being family is hard work. More times than not, we fail. Nevertheless, you sent us help. Lighting our way are the faces of your Holy Family. Through the divine treasure of your mother, Mary, we learn the nature of total love and commitment. She lived love as well as the virtue of humility and that of faithful trust and obedience in God. Your earthly father, Joseph, heeding his calls accepted the full responsibility of manhood and became the protector of the family. Hard working and righteous, he was indeed a good man who held steadfast to his faith. Moreover, you grew in the bounty of their grace-filled love. You grew within the Father's watchful eye and as we learn to accept this wondrous gift born of mystery, we offer our thanksgiving. To live family life is to live within the center of life itself. For it is there that choice is born and holiness determined.

A Reading

Peace and war begin at home. If we truly want peace in the world, let us begin by loving one another in our own families. If we want to spread joy, we need every family to have joy.[1]

Psalm Response

Oh Lord, let the light of your countenance shine upon us!
You put gladness into my heart,
more than when grain and wine abound,
As soon as I lie down, I fall peacefully asleep,
for you alone, O Lord,
bring security to my dwelling.
Amen.
      Ps 4:7-9

The Challenge

Think about your family. Do you pray together? Are you preserving traditions?

Think about each family member. See them within their holiness. Use St. Paul's definition (Col 3, 12-15). Share a positive affirmation with each member of your family. What was their response?

Do you perceive your family to include members from both sides of the preceding generation? What is your commitment to them? Does it need to change?

The Baptism of Jesus

Scripture

Then Jesus came from Galilee to John at the Jordan to be baptized by him. John tried to prevent him, saying, "I need to be baptized by you, and yet you are coming to me?" Jesus said to him in reply, "Allow it now, for thus it is fitting for us to fulfill all righteousness." Then he allowed him. After Jesus was baptized he came up from the water and behold, the heavens were opened (for him), and he saw the Spirit of God descending like a dove (and) coming upon him. And a voice came from the heavens saying, "This is my beloved Son, with whom I am well pleased."
    Matthew 3:13-17

Thoughts

O Incarnate One

From the beginning of time the mystery of the Trinity remains an enigma embodied in your coming. Yet, in the luminous light of your baptism, believers are graced with understanding. The Father, Son and Holy Spirit, three persons yet one, forever is shaping our faith so that we might become one with God. All is indeed ... grace. All is the treasure of your everlasting love and of your Divine Plan. Within our own baptism we are graced by *the Father who has made ... (us) ... fit to share in the inheritance of the holy ones in light. He delivered us from the power of darkness and transferred us to the kingdom of his beloved Son, in whom we have redemption, the forgiveness of sins"* (Col 1:12, 13). Our soul now imprinted in the baptism of love enables each of us to be readied for life's journey.

A Reading

Those whom God has foreknown, He has also predestined to become conformed to the image of His divine Son ... And those whom He has predestined, He has also called; and those whom He has called He has also justified; and those whom

He has justified, He has also glorified. What then shall we say after that? If God is for us, who can be against us? Who will separate me from the love of Christ? (Rom 8:29-31, 35). Yes, we have become His through baptism, that is what Paul means by these words: *He called them*; yes called to receive the seal of the Holy Trinity; at the same time we have been made, in the words of St. Peter, *sharers in the divine nature,* (2 Pet 1:14) we have received *a beginning of His existence* (Heb 3:14). Then, He has justified us by His sacraments by His direct "touches" in our contemplation "in the depths" of our soul; justified as also by faith and according to the measure of our faith in the redemption that Jesus Christ has acquired for us. ... He wants to glorify us, and for that reason, says St. Paul, He *"has made us worthy to share in the inheritance of the saints in light"* (Col 1:12), but we will be glorified in the measure in which we will have been conformed to the image of His divine Son. ... So let us contemplate this adored image, let us remain unceasingly under its radiance so that it may imprint itself on us; let us go to everything with the same attitude of soul that our holy Master would have. Then we will realize the great plan by which God has *"resolved in Himself to restore all things in Christ* (Eph 1:9-10).[1]

Psalm Response

Come; let us sing joyfully to the Lord;
let us acclaim the Rock of our salvation.
Let us greet him with thanksgiving
let us joyfully sing psalms to him
For the Lord is a great God,
And a great king above all gods.
In his hands are the depths of the earth
and the tops of the mountains are his.
His is the sea, for he has made it,
And the dry land, which his hands have formed.

Come let us bow down in worship
 let us kneel before the Lord who made us.
For he is our God,
And we are the people he Shepherd's,
 the flock he guides.
Amen.
    Psalm 95:1-7

THE CHALLENGE

Have you witnessed the working of the Blessed Trinity in your life? Won't you share this wonderful gift with another?

A Lesson from the Beloved

Scripture

The Scribes and the Pharisees brought a woman who had been caught in adultery and made her stand in the middle. They said to him, "Teacher, this woman was caught in the very act of committing adultery. Now in the law, Moses commanded us to stone such a woman. So what do you say?" They said this to test him so that they could have some charge to bring against him, Jesus bent down and began to write on the ground with his finger. But when they continued asking him, he straightened up and said to them, "Let the one among you who is without sin be the first to throw a stone at her." Again he bent down and wrote on the ground. And in response, then went away one by one, beginning with the elders. So he was left alone with the woman before him. Then Jesus straightened up and said to her. "Woman where are they? Has no one condemned you?" She replied, "No one Sir." Then Jesus said, "neither do I condemn you. Go and from now on do not sin anymore."
    John 8:1-11

Thoughts

Beloved Jesus

You are Love itself. You call each of us to love you, our Savior and Triune God. You also are calling us to love our neighbors as ourselves. It is in the comfort of your Divine Heart that one begins to experience the depth of your unconditional love. You clothe us with grace and our wounded self rests. We are loved by you and forgiven for our sins. What you ask of us, is to *be merciful even as your Father is. Forgive and you will be forgiven* (Luke 6:36, 37). You ask, "*why do you notice the splinter in your brother's eye, but do not perceive the wooden beam in your own?*" (Luke 6:41). If we accept the challenge to look inward, we are gifted with a new eye that beholds our own shadow-making faults and we begin to experience your ever present mercy. It is your living love that heals our brokenness and frees the soul to accept the self as it is. With this gift our compassion is kindled. The soul now humbled understands and accepts the frailty of its own human condition. We have learned that if we are to live in your presence our actions count. We now know we can never assume we truly love you, if we judge another.

A Reading

Reality is the first principle of truth. To be human means to remain connected to our humanness and to reality. It means to abandon the loneliness of being closed up in illusions, dreams and ideologies, frightened of reality and to choose to move toward connectedness. To be human is to accept ourselves just as we are with our own history as it is and to work without fear toward a greater openness, greater understanding and a greater love of others. The truth will set us free only if we let it penetrate our heart and rend the veil that separates head from heart. It is important not only to join the head and the heart but to love truth, to let it inspire our lives, our attitudes and our way of living. The truth of religion and morality shows itself when ... (it) ... liberates us and gives us a deep respect and compassion for others.[1]

Psalm Response

I am bound, O God, by vows to you;
your thank offerings I will fulfill.
For you have rescued me from death,
my feet, too, from stumbling;
that I may walk before God in the
light of the living.
Amen.
      Psalm 56:13, 14

The Challenge

What is your reaction to Jesus' lesson?

The Call to Faith

CLOCKWISE: *Jesus and Nicodemus; The Samaritan Woman; Jesus Encounters the Blind Man; The Raising of Lazarus.*

Scripture

Now there was a Pharisee named Nicodemus, a ruler of the Jews. He came to Jesus at night and said to him, "Rabbi, we know that you are a teacher who has come from God for no one can do theses signs that you are doing unless God is with him." Jesus answered.. "Amen, amen, I say to you, no one can see the kingdom of God without being born from above." Nicodemus said to him, " How can a person once grown old be born again? Surely he cannot reenter his mother's womb and be born again, can he?" Jesus answered, "Amen, amen, I say to you, no one can enter the kingdom of God without being born of water and Spirit. What is born of flesh is flesh and what is born of spirit is spirit. Do not be amazed that I told you, 'You must be born from above.' The wind blows where it wills, and you can hear the sound it makes, but you do not know where it comes from or where it goes; so it is with everyone who is born of the Spirit."

    John 3:1-8

... Jesus tired from his journey, sat down at the well. It was about noon. A woman of Samaria came to draw water. Jesus said to her, "Give me a drink." His disciples had gone into the town to buy food. The Samaritan woman said to him, "How can you, a Jew, ask me, a Samaritan woman, for a drink?" (For Jews use nothing in common with Samaritans.) Jesus answered and said to her, "If you knew the gift of God and who is saying to you, 'give me a drink,' you would have asked him and he would have given you living water." (The woman) said to him "Sir, you do not even have a bucket and the cistern is deep; where then can you get this living water? Are you greater than our Father Jacob, who gave us this cistern and drank from it himself with his children and his flocks?" Jesus answered and said to her, "Everyone who drinks this water will be thirsty again; but whoever drinks the water I shall give will never thirst, the water I shall give will become in him a spring of water welling up to eternal life." The woman said to him, "Sir, give me this water, so that I may not be thirsty or have to keep coming here to draw water."

    John 4:6-15

Now there is in Jerusalem at the Sheep (Gate) a pool called in Hebrew Bethesda, with five porticos. In these lay a large number of ill, blind, lame and crippled. One man was there who had been ill for thirty-eight years, When Jesus saw him lying there and knew that he head been ill for a long time, he said to him, "Do you want to be well?" The sick man answered him, "Sir, I have no one to put me in the pool when the water is stirred up. While I am on my way someone else gets down there before me." Jesus said to him, "Rise, take up your mat, and walk." Immediately the man became well, took up his mat and walked.
    John 5:2-8

When Jesus arrived, he found that Lazarus had already been in the tomb for four days. Now Bethany was near Jerusalem only about two miles away. And many of the Jews had come to Martha and Mary to comfort them about their brother. When Martha heard that Jesus was coming she went to meet him, but Mary sat at home. Martha said to Jesus, "Lord, if you had been here, my brother would not have died. (But) even now I know that whatever you ask of God, God will give you." Jesus said to her, "Your brother will rise." Martha said to him, "I know he will rise in the resurrection on the last day." Jesus told her, "I am the resurrection and the life; whoever believes in me even if he dies will live and everyone who lives and believes in me will never die. Do you believe this?" She said to him, "Yes Lord, I have come to believe that you are the Messiah, the Son of God, the one who is coming to save the world."

When she had said this, she went and called her sister Mary ... . When Mary came to where Jesus was and saw him, she fell at his feet and said to him, "Lord if you had been here my brother would not have died." When Jesus saw her weeping and the Jews who had come with her weeping, he be came perturbed and deeply trouble and said, "Where have you laid him?" So Jesus ... came to the tomb. It was a cave and a stone lay across it. Jesus said, "Take away the stone." ... So they took away the stone. And Jesus raised his eyes and said, "Father, I thank you for hearing me. I know that you always hear me, but because of the crowd here I have said this, that they may believe that you sent me." And when he had said this, he cried out in a loud voice, "Lazarus, come out!"

The dead man came out, tied hand and foot with burial bands, and his face was wrapped in a cloth. So Jesus said to them "Untie him and let him go."
  John 11:17, 28, 32-34, 38, 41-44

THOUGHTS

Beloved Jesus

Woven within the fabric of these scripture readings is a single golden thread that links each with the other. It is the call to faith. A call that carries with it a thirst so profound it can only be quenched when served the cup of living water. Where darkness once prevailed, the living flame of your heart now nourishes the soul. The way is illuminated. You see, the road is now graced with living stones etched in Love.[1]

A READING

There are movements of the soul deeper than words can describe and yet more powerful than any reason, which can give a man to know beyond question or arguing or doubt that "digitus Dei est hic (the finger of God is here)" and the name of that reality is grace. God does inspire man by his grace, does lift the heart, does enlighten the mind and move the will. Faith is required to accept that reality, but it is a reality nonetheless.[2]

PSALM RESPONSE

How lovely is your dwelling place,
O Lord of hosts!
My soul yearns and pines for the courts of the Lord.
My heart and my flesh
Cry out for the living God.

Happy they who dwell in your house!
Continually they praise you.
Happy the men whose strength you are!
Their hearts are set upon the pilgrimage. ...

O Lord of hosts, hear my prayer
Harken, O God of Jacob.
O God, behold our shield,
And look upon the face of your anointed.
I had rather one day in your courts
Than a thousand elsewhere. ...
Amen.
   Psalm 84:2, 3, 5, 6, 9-11

THE CHALLENGE

How have you centered your faith? Has there ever been a time that you experienced doubt? What did you do about it?

Have you ever helped strengthen another person's belief? Do you realize in that encounter you were evangelizing?

The Transfiguration

Scripture

After six days Jesus took Peter, James and John, his brother, and led them up a high mountain by themselves. And he was transfigured before them; his face shone like the sun and his clothes became white as light. And behold, Moses and Elijah appeared to be conversing with him. Then Peter said to Jesus in reply, "Lord it is good that we are here. If you wish, I will make three tents here, one for you, one for Moses and one for Elijah. While he was still speaking, behold, a bright cloud cast a shadow over them, then from the cloud came a voice that said, "This is my beloved Son, with whom I am well pleased; listen to him." When the disciples heard this, they fell prostrate and were very much afraid. But Jesus came and touched them, saying, "Rise, and do not be afraid." And when the disciples raised their eyes, they saw no one else but Jesus alone.
  Matthew 17:1-8

Thoughts

Abba

You came in that radiant, luminous cloud to declare the divinity of your son, Jesus, and in that mystery of light, the Apostles heard your voice declaring, *"Here is my servant whom I uphold, My chosen one."* Could it be at that very moment, the Apostles might have also remembered that other time in Caesarea when your Son asked them *"who do people say I am?"* and they replied *"John the Baptist, others Elijah, still others, one of the prophets"*? Again your Son asked, *"But who do you say I am?"* Peter said in reply, *"You are the Messiah"* (Mark 8:29) Now ... high on Mount Tabor, the glory of your Godhead shines forth on your beloved Son who is flanked by Moses and Elijah; his face shining in brilliant light! And when the Apostles heard your voice, they fell prostrate to the ground and were filled with fear. In that extraordinary moment, the messianic hope for all mankind was realized; for Moses and Elijah were speaking *of his exodus that he was going to accomplish in Jerusalem* (Luke 9:30, 31). There in the light of the Transfiguration stood the Pascal Lamb whose death and resurrection was to follow in fulfillment of your love for all of us.

It is in the mystery of The Transfiguration that one's heart is radically exposed to that gateway "where all things shine with divine radiance, where there is joy and gladness and exultation: where there is nothing in our hearts but peace, serenity and stillness … . For here, in our hearts, Christ takes up his abode together with the Father, saying as he enters: '*Today, salvation has come to this house.*'"[1] Now … we know … never to forget, the divine vision of the Transfiguration, prefigures the Paschal mystery and captures for all time, the luminous gift of Love."[2,3] And, from this gift, we learn its meaning when we selflessly serve others. We learn "with God, man 'creates' the world; with God, man 'creates' his personal salvation."[4]

A Reading

Just as we must be baptized with Jesus and hear the voice calling us to serve others … so must we also participate in the experience of Jesus as we visit our own mount of the Transfiguration. This may occur in a dramatic moment … but it is more likely to happen over a period of time. The evidence for this will be a gradual awareness that the most important thing in life may not be winning little victories that make sense in a secular world. … When all is said and done our record of unselfish love will be the only thing that really matters.[5]

Psalm Response

The Lord's revelation to my Master:
"Sit on my right:
your foes I will put beneath your feet"

The Lord will wield from Zion
Your scepter of power:
rule in the midst of all your foes.

A prince from the day of your birth

On the holy mountains;
From the womb before the dawn I begot you.
The Lord has sworn an oath he will not change.
"You are a priest for ever,
a priest like Melchizdek of old."

The Master standing at your right hand
will shatter kings in the day of his great wrath.

He shall drink from the stream by the wayside
and therefore he shall lift up his head.
Amen
    Psalm 110:1-5, 7[6]

THE CHALLENGE

Revisit the scripture image. Notice the Greek cross and X monogram. Do you see the nails? Read Luke 9:30,31. What does the scripture symbolize for you?

The Agony in the Garden

Scripture

Then Jesus came with them to a place called Gethsemane and he said to his disciples, "Sit here, while I go over there and pray." He took along Peter and the two sons of Zebedee, and began to feel sorrow and distressed. Then he said to them "My soul is sorrowful even to death. Remain here and keep watch with me." He advanced a little and fell prostrate in prayer, saying, "My Father, if it is possible, let this cup pass from me; yet, not as I will, but as you will." When he returned to his disciples he found them asleep. He said to Peter, "So you could not keep watch with me for one hour? Watch and pray that you may not undergo the test. The spirit is willing, but the flesh is weak." Withdrawing a second time, he prayed again, "My Father, if it is not possible that this cup pass without my drinking it, your will be done!" Then he returned once more and found them asleep, for they could not keep their eyes open. He left them again and withdrew again and prayed a third time, saying the same thing again. Then he return to his disciples and said to them, "Are you still sleeping and taking your rest? Behold, the hour is at hand when the Son of Man is to be handed over to sinners. Get up, let us go, look my betrayer is at hand.
  Matthew 26:36-46

Thoughts

Beloved Jesus

You asked Peter and the two sons of Zebedee to "watch and pray" with you. Yet the three disciples could not stay awake. It was as if night had enveloped them. A night darkened by the threat of all that was to come. A night filled with penetrating fear and grief. A night so terrible, they could only sleep.

Yet, you asked your disciples to watch and pray with you because you knew hope is centered in prayer.[1] You understood prayer prepares the soul to meet the challenges of life. Watch and pray with me. Take your stand with me. Be a "watchtower of faith."[2] Your call to your disciples was a call for each of us; to remember to stand the post, to prepare for the unknown through prayer. To be mindful of The Father and realize that when we pray into the darkness, we have the ability to learn God exists in all that is.³ When we stand with our Creator, we begin to comprehend the meaning and depth of his divine plan. It is our opportunity to be faithful and ... *trust in the Lord forever. For the Lord is an eternal Rock* (Isa 26:4).

Through prayer we are gifted with fortitude. We learn you are always with us especially during the darkest of times. No longer need we be bound in fear. Prayer gives us strength to meet all life's demands, to strive forward with the Father's resolve.⁴

With the gift of prayer, we are graced in faith and empowered to surrender our will. It is our faith in you, Jesus, that infuses us with courage and hope. It is you who calls each of us to be faithful in all circumstances.

Yet ... the Beloved prayed alone in the garden of Gethsemane. And, as he sought the will of the Father *an angel from heaven appeared to strengthen him. He was in such agony and he prayed so fervently that his sweat became like drops of blood falling on the ground* (Luke 22:43-44). Still, Jesus accepted his Father's will. He knew through his death and resurrection he would be giving us life ... even in death.

A Reading

See yourself in Him.

If you have trials to bear, if you are sorrowful watch Him on His way to the garden, What grief must have arisen in His soul to cause Him, who was patience itself to manifest and complain of it!

Or see Him bound to the column, full of sufferings. His flesh all torn to pieces because of His tender love for you.

Or look on Him with the cross and not allowed to stay to take a breath. He will gaze on you with beautiful compassionate eyes and forget his own grief to solace yours, only because you went to comfort Him and turned to look at Him.⁵

Psalm Response

O most High, when I begin to fear
in you I will trust.
In God, in whose promise I glory,
in God I trust without fear... .
Amen.
      Psalm 56:5

The Challenge

What do the words "watch and pray" mean to you?

The Way of the Cross

Thoughts and Scripture

The Way of the Cross, is the story of your Passion. It is a devotion that has been practiced over time. It is an opportunity to meet life at its core and be transformed. It is an invitation to seek Truth and face the self, with a new sense of reality and completeness. For "… you (our Redeemer) share the lot of all of us; i.e., the way of a dying humanity."[1] The Way of the Cross stirs the soul to search for the meaning of life, death, suffering and sin and as we center you within ourselves; we also learn we have this wondrous opportunity to transform our own death, because of your sacred saving act. The Way of the Cross, your Passion, is a journey that transcends time, leaving the witness centered in the moment and then confronted by the measure of his or her relationship with you and its obligations. The Way of the Cross, is your grace filled gift to all of us; our gateway to salvation.

> *The hour has come for the Son of man to be glorified. Amen, Amen, I say to you, unless a grain of wheat falls to the ground and dies, it remains a grain of wheat but if it dies, it produces much fruit. I am troubled now, yet, what should I say Father save me from this hour? But it was for this purpose that I came to this hour. Father, glorify your name" Then a voice came from heaven "I have glorified it and will glorify it again. The crowd heard it and said it was thunder, but others said, "…an angel has spoken to him" Jesus answered and said. "This voice did not come for my sake, but for yours, now is the time of judgment in this world. And when I am lifted up from the earth, I will draw everyone to myself."*
>   John 12:23, 24, 27-32

Your trust Beloved in the Divine Plan is heard within that thunder. You neither turned away, nor questioned your Father's will. You understood what it meant to willingly surrender.[2] Yet, for those of us who gaze upon you and hear your Word, we cannot help but wonder and then realize … you came into the world within a Divine Mystery that recognized obedience and trust as a part of the other. You, The Messiah, came to expose us to your Word, to the Law of Love and to teach us to seek and obey your Father's Will.[3] You understood we had to learn *that all things work for good for those who love God, who are called according to his purpose* (Rom 8:28). We had to learn when one seeks the Father's will in conformity with He who is Love, trust evolves with a certain sense of just "simply knowing." So it was that you, The Son of Man, The Suffering Servant of Yahweh, High Priest and Victim voluntarily gave up your life as an offering for sin. *Who would believe what we have heard? He grew up like a sapling before him, like a shoot from the parched earth; there was in him no stately bearing to make us look at him, He was spurned and avoided by men a man of suffering accustomed to infirmity. Yet it was our infirmities that he bore, our sufferings that he endured. But he was pierced for our offenses, crushed for our sins* (Isa 53:1-5). It is this prophesy from the Old Testament that brings to fore what every generation must bear ... that you, Beloved Jesus, died for our sins. ... *Just as Moses lifted up the serpent in the desert, so must the Son of Man be lifted up, so that everyone who believes in (you) may have eternal life* (John 3:14, 15).

THE STATIONS OF THE CROSS

1. Jesus Is Condemned To Death

Now Jesus stood before the governor and he questioned him, "Are you the King of the Jews?" Jesus said, "You say so." And when he was accused by the chief priest and elders he made no answer. Then Pilate said to him, "Do you not hear how many things they are testifying against you?" But he did not answer him one word ... Now on the occasion of the feast the governor was accustomed to release to the crowd one prisoner whom they wished, and at that time they had a notorious prisoner called Barabbas. So when they had assembled, Pilate said to them, " which one do you want me to release to you ... Barabbas, or Jesus called the Messiah?" The chief priests and the elders persuaded the crowds to ask for Barabbas, but to destroy Jesus. Pilate then said to them "Then what shall I do with Jesus called Messiah? They all said, "Let him be crucified."... Pilate took water and washed his hands in the sight of the crowd, saying " I am innocent of this man's blood. Look to it yourselves." Then he released Barabbas to them, but after he had Jesus scourged, he handed him over to be crucified (Matt 27:11-13, 15-17, 22, 24, 26).

When Pilate chose to dissociate himself from the decision by symbolically washing his hands; the deed was done. You Beloved, were condemned to die and your people; the Jews collectively bore the guilt of your death. Although there were those over the centuries, in the great councils of the Church who exhorted their people to recognize their own sin, they did not do so.[4] It is always easier to blame another than find fault within ourselves. Yet, the Church persisted and "declared at Second Vatican Council, that neither all Jews indiscriminately at that time, nor Jews today, could be charged with the crimes committed during the Passion. The Jews should never be spoken of as rejected or accursed as if this followed from holy Scripture."[5] It was understood we are the ones who are guilty. It is our sins that made the Lord Christ suffer the torment of the cross. It is we who crucify the Son of God anew."[6]

2. Jesus Accepts His Cross

So they took Jesus and carrying the cross himself he went out to what is called the Place of the Skull, in Hebrew, Golgotha" (John 19:17)... *"Like a lamb led to slaughter."* (Isa 53:7).

The Chosen People had turned away from their obligations to the covenant and for this reason you were sent to us. Faith is a grace that can only be received when one accepts salvation as God's righteousness. So it was that your acceptance of The Cross was your assent on behalf of all humanity to be the living sacrifice. *It is the power of God for the salvation of everyone who believes: for Jew first, and then Greek. For in it is revealed the righteousness of God from faith to faith; as it is written, "The one who is righteous by faith will live"* (Rom 1:16, 17). This is your gift ... a renewed relationship built upon love and the power of forgiveness. What you ask from us is simply that we center you within our hearts. If we are to live out our lives in active consent of your sacred covenant, we need you, Beloved Jesus, to save us from our wounded selves. We need your help to live out your standard of moral values that promote the dignity and worth of all people. We need you, to save us from our self-centeredness and the harshness of a heart that is unforgiving. We shall never forget ... *it was our infirmities that (you) bore, our sufferings that (you) endured* (Isa 53:4).

3. Jesus Falls The First Time

In quite and in trust your strength lies (Isa 30:15). It is no wonder you have fallen, for you are carrying the weight of all our failings. Yet, *(you are) silent and opened not (your) mouth* (Isa 53:7). As you struggle to rise we see the strength of your will to fulfill your Father's Divine Plan. Seeing you suffer, yet so determined, empowers us to remember, if we surrender our will, we too will have the opportunity to be filled with a new sense of strength and courage. We are strongest, when we are one with The Father's Will.

4. Jesus Meets His Mother

And you yourself a sword will pierce so that the thoughts of many hearts may be revealed (Luke 2:35). There she is ... your Mother. She is with the other woman of Galilee and the disciple called John. She is standing so still, so full of love and grief. One cannot help but recall the day you were presented in the Temple ... As Simeon blessed you and your parents, he said, *"Behold this child is destined for the fall and rise of many in Israel ... to be a sign that will be contradicted"* (Luke 2:34). It was then he prophesied about your Mother and it too has come to pass. Your Mother has become for us 'our Lady' who understands all that is in our heart. For the reality is on this same day long ago, two hearts bled, as both were but a part of the other.

5. Simon of Cyrene Helps Jesus Carry His Cross

As they led him away they took hold of a certain Simon a Cyrenian who was coming in from the country and after laying the cross on him, they made him carry it behind Jesus (Luke 23:26).

To understand the meaning of life, each of us must shoulder not only our own crosses, but help others to carry theirs. To be your disciple, is to know "Christ is counting on you ... on me ... on all of us."[7] To help another, is to walk in the light of your love.

6. Veronica Wipes The Face Of Jesus

Then the righteous will answer him and say, "Lord, when did we see you hungry and feed you, or thirsty and give you drink?" (Matt 25:37). What do you do for the least among you? It is easy to say one is a believer; yet another to actualize our belief. It is in our actions, that our commitment to you is tested. When truth becomes relative, values become undifferentiated.[8] How do we live out our faith in our home, our neighborhood and in the workplace? Are we living in friendship with those among us? Do we offer ourselves to someone in need as did Veronica? If we are to be enkindled within your light my Lord, one must be clothed in your Christ centered values. To live otherwise is to turn away from you.

7. Jesus Falls The Second Time

But then, how would scripture be fulfilled which says, *it must come to pass in this way* (Matt 26:54). *I am wearied ...* (Ps 6:7). See He is falling a second time. It is difficult to pull oneself up time and again. Yet, as difficult as it was He pulled himself up. Though we may even fall into sin, the reality is, we can be filled with resolve to pull ourselves upward. You my Lord knew you were not alone and neither are we. With you Jesus everything becomes possible. *All this has come to pass that the writing of the prophets may be fulfilled* (Matt 26:56).

8. Jesus Comforts the Women of Jerusalem

A large crowd of people followed Jesus, including many women who mourned and lamented him. Jesus turned to them and said, "Daughters of Jerusalem, do not weep for me; weep instead for yourselves and for your children, for indeed the days are coming when people will say, Blessed are the barren the wombs that never bore and breasts that never nursed" (Luke 23:27, 28).

Do you remember the words of the Psalmist? *Be still and know that I am God* (Ps 46:10).[9] You my Lord stopped and shared your concern for the Daughters of Jerusalem. You knew all that was to befall them. In times of adversity, do we remember we can always turn to you ... our place of "refuge and strength?"[10]

9. Jesus Falls the Third Time

He began to teach them the Son of Man must suffer greatly and be rejected by the elders, the chief priest and the scribes and be killed and rise after three days. He spoke this openly (Mark 8:31).

Although Divine, you, my Lord, came to us in human form and now you are suffering because of us. We, who gaze upon you, have no choice but to hide our eyes. We are filled with remorse. We now know, you have humbled yourself out of obedience to your Father's will and have done so on our behalf.

10. Jesus Is Stripped Of His Clothing

... when they mocked him, they stripped him ... (Mark 20). And as they did, one realizes, the soul can only be whole when one empties the self and surrenders completely to your will. You, Beloved Jesus, were sent for us to discover the true meaning of obedience. Your mission; our salvation. You were stripped of everything, except your heart, which is filled with mercy and we are humbled by your love for us. *Through his suffering my servant shall justify many, and their guilt he shall bear. ... He shall take away the sins of many, and win pardon for their offenses* (Isa 53:11,12).

11. Jesus Is Nailed To The Cross

... They crucified him and the criminals there, one on his right and the other on his left. Then Jesus said, "Father, forgive them, they know not what they do" (Luke 23:34). *... When Jesus saw his mother and the disciple whom he loved, he said to His mother, "Woman, behold your son." Then he said to the disciple, "Behold your mother." And from that hour the disciple took her into his home"* (John 19:26).

The final hour is upon us. Though the light is dim we see you hanging from that tree, crucified and in excruciating pain. Yet, there you are calling upon The Father to forgive us ... we who caused your suffering. Then ... in a most tender moment, you presented your Mother and your beloved Disciple to each other and taught us the importance of caring for each other.

12. Jesus Dies On The Cross

"From noon onward, darkness came over the whole land until three in the afternoon. And about three o'clock Jesus cried out in a loud voice. "Eli, Eli, lema sabachthani?" which means, "My God, my God, why have you forsaken me?" Some of the bystanders who heard it said, "This one is calling for Elijah." Immediately one of them ran to get a sponge; he soaked it in wine and putting it on a reed gave it to him to drink. But the rest said, "Wait, let us see if Elijah come to save him," But Jesus cried out again in a loud voice and gave up his spirit. And behold, the veil of the sanctuary was torn in two from top to bottom. The earth quaked, rocks were split, tombs were opened and the bodies of many saints who had fallen asleep were raised (Matt 27:45-52).

In the fullness of that terrible moment a great sadness descended upon those who knew and loved you. Though there were those who never quite comprehended the magnitude of your deed; we are brought to our knees, as we recall the psalmist's words, *You who fear the Lord, praise him; all you descendants of Jacob, give glory to him; revere him all you descendants of Israel"* (Ps 22:24-25). And, as the heavens quaked, they knew, the mighty arm of the Holiest of the Holy was upon them. The promise was now forever fulfilled. By surrendering your life in obedience to your Father's will, we human kind received, in that terrible moment, the outpouring of your salvific love. By your suffering and death on the cross, you struck evil at its core and redeemed mankind for all eternity. By taking on the sins of mankind and those of the world, sin was conquered. In dying, you gave us eternal salvation and with it eternal life. By shedding your precious blood on the Cross, we are healed in the outpouring of your Divine Love. In your humanity, you sought to teach us to surrender our will as you had, with enduring faith. You taught us the limits of our humanity and we learned that if we cling to you while embracing the crosses in our own lives; our soul will begin to comprehend that it is never alone. It is in suffering that we recall we are the branches of your vine and that you will never abandon us. Darkness no longer can permeate the essence of our soul. Your gift of Divine Love is our transcendent gateway through which we can all offer up in prayer our own sufferings on behalf of others; uniting our sufferings with those that you experienced while hanging on the Cross. It is in our suffering that we, your loved ones, have the opportunity to live out our humanity in the fullness of our soul with you, Our Suffering Servant and Redeemer.

13. Jesus Is Taken Down From The Cross

And… as you were taken down from the cross and placed in your Mother's arms, one could almost hear from somewhere deep inside the *dust, the dying groan and the souls of the wounded cry out* as the final sword pierced her heart (Job 24:12).

14. The Body Of Jesus Is Laid In The Tomb

When it was evening there came a rich man from Arimathea named Joseph, who was himself a disciple of Jesus. He went to Pilate and asked for the body of Jesus; then Pilate ordered it to be handed over. Taking the body, Joseph wrapped it in clean linen and laid it in his new tomb that he had hewn in the rock. Then he rolled a huge stone across the entrance of the tomb and departed. But Mary Magdalene and the other Mary remained sitting there, facing the tomb (Matt 27:57-61).

It is finished!

A Reading

Christ suffered without sin on his hands for he committed no sin and deceit was not found on his lips. Yet he suffered the pain of the cross for our redemption. His prayer to God was pure, his alone out of all mankind, for in the midst of his suffering he prayed for his persecutors. Father forgive them, for they do not know what they are doing.

Is it possible to offer or even to imagine, a purer kind of prayer than that which shows mercy to one's torturers by making intercession for them? It was thanks to this kind of prayer that the frenzied persecutors who shed the blood of our Redeemer drank it afterward in faith and proclaimed him to be the Son of God.

The text goes on fittingly to speak of Christ's blood. Earth, do not cover over my blood, do not let my cry find a hiding place in you. When each man sinned, God had said: Earth you are, and to earth you will return. Earth does not cover over the blood of our Redeemer, for every sinner, as he drinks the blood that is the price of his redemption offers praise and thanksgiving, and to the best of his power makes that blood known to all around him.

Earth has not hidden away his blood, for holy church has preached in every corner of the world the mystery of its redemption.

Notice what follows: Do not let my cry find a hiding place in you. The blood is drunk, the blood of redemption, is itself the cry of our Redeemer. Paul speaks of the sprinkled blood that calls out more eloquently than Abel's. Of Abel's blood scripture had written: The voice of your brother's blood cries out to me from the earth. The blood of Jesus calls out more eloquently than Abel's for the blood of Abel asked for the death of Cain the fratricide, while the blood of the Lord has asked for, and obtained life for his persecutors.

If the sacrament of the Lord's passion is to work its effect in us, we must imitate what we receive and proclaim to mankind what we revere. The cry of the Lord finds a hiding place in us if our lips fail to speak of this, though our hearts believe in it. So that his cry may not lie concealed in us it remains for us all, each in his own measure, to make known to those around us the mystery of our new life in Christ.[11, 12]

PSALM RESPONSE

The Lord is my Shepard, I shall not want
In verdant pastures he gives me repose.
Beside restful waters he leads me, he refreshes my soul
He guides me in right paths for his name's sake
Even though I walk in the dark valley
I fear no evil; for you are at my side
With your rod and staff
that gives me courage.

You spread the table before me in the sight of my foes
You anoint my head with oil; my cup overflows
Only goodness and kindness follow me
All the days of my life;
And I shall dwell in the house of the Lord
For years to come.
Amen.
    Psalm 23

THE CHALLENGE

Be still ... and remember!

The Empty Tomb

Scripture

On the first day of the week, Mary of Magdala came to the tomb early in the morning, while it was still dark, and saw the stone removed from the tomb. So she ran and went to Simon Peter and to the other disciple whom Jesus loved, and told them, "They have taken the Lord from the tomb and we don't know where they put him." So Peter and the other disciple went out and came to the tomb. They both ran, but the other disciple ran faster than Peter and arrived at the tomb first; he bent down and saw the burial cloths there, but did not go in. When Simon Peter arrived after him, he went into the tomb and saw the burial cloths there, and the cloth that had covered his head, not with the burial cloths but rolled up in a separate place. Then the other disciple also went in, the one who had arrived at the tomb first, and he saw and believed. For they did not yet understand the scripture that he had to rise from the dead. Then the disciples returned home.
     John 20:1-10

Thoughts

O Holiest of Holy

He is risen! And with these words a Divine light was lit deep inside the far reaches of our universe. Death was destroyed by the power of love.[1] *All the ends of the earth shall remember and turn to the Lord; All the families of the nations shall bow down before him. For dominion is the Lord's and he rules the nations. To him alone shall bow down all who sleep in the earth* (Ps 22:28-30).

In your dying, Beloved Jesus, the new covenant was inscribed forever within the hearts of mankind. For it was said, "*I will place my law within them and write it upon their hearts; I will be their God and they shall be my people. All from the least to the greatest shall k*now *me,*" says the Lord, "*for I forgive their evildoing and remember their sin no more*" (Jer 31:33-34). Your sacrifice, Beloved Jesus, was the gift of salvation, the gift of life. Mankind "loses everything in death except God and in this way achieves blessedness."[2] As we face our own mortality, we need no longer fear the unknown, but rather celebrate what will be a new birth, a new awakening into the heart of the Beloved ...

A Reading

On the third day, the friends of Christ coming at day-break to the place found the grave empty and the stone rolled away. In varying ways, they realized the new wonder; but even they hardly realized that the world had died in the night. What they were looking at was the first day of a new creation, with a new heaven and a new earth; and in a semblance of the Gardener, God walked again in the garden, in the cool not of the evening, but of the dawn.[3]

Psalm Response

Sing to the Lord a new song;
sing to the Lord, all you lands,
Sing to the Lord; bless his name;
announce his salvation, day after day,
Tell his glory among the nations;
among all peoples, his wondrous deeds.

For great is the Lord and highly to be praised;
awesome is he, beyond all gods.
For all the gods of the nations are things of naught
but the Lord made the heavens.
Splendor and majesty go before him;
praise and grandeur are in his sanctuary.

Give to the Lord, you families of nations,
give to the Lord glory and praise;
Give to the Lord the glory due his name!
Bring gifts, and enter his courts;
worship the Lord in holy attire.
Tremble before him, all the earth;
say among the nations: The Lord is king.

He has made the world firm, not to be moved;
he governs the peoples with equity.

Let the heavens be glad and the earth rejoice;
let the sea and what fills it resound;
let the plains be joyful and all that is in them!
Then shall all the trees of the forest
exult before the Lord, for he comes;
for he comes to rule the earth
He shall rule the world with justice
and the peoples with his constancy.
Amen.
    Psalm 96 1-13

THE CHALLENGE

Compose a prayer of Praise and Thanksgiving.

The Martyrdom of Stephen

Scripture

When they heard this, they were infuriated and they ground their teeth at him. But he, filled with the holy Spirit looked up intently to heaven and saw the glory of God and Jesus standing at the right hand of God. And he said, "Behold, I see the heavens opened and the Son of Man standing at the right hand of God." But they cried out in a loud voice, covered their ears and rushed upon him together. They threw him out of the city and began to stone him. The witnesses laid down their cloaks at the feet of a young man named Saul. As they were stoning Stephen, he called out, "Lord Jesus, receive my spirit." Then he fell to his knees and cried out in a loud voice, "Lord, do not hold this sin against them," and when he said this, he fell asleep.
Acts 7:54-60

Thoughts

Abba

You did not give us a spirit of cowardice, but rather of power and love (2 Tim 1:7). Indeed you "use humanity to save humanity."[1] Did you not give us your only son, who in his humanity died for our salvation? It was your son, Jesus, who taught us while hanging on the cross true love carries with it acts of forgiveness. St. Stephen, the first Christian martyr, died giving witness to this cornerstone of our faith and throughout time others have followed in his footsteps. Each is treasured, their witness, a guiding light.

Though a scourge of evil has left its mark upon our shores, we remember the heroic efforts of the Passengers of Flight 93. One of those passengers was a young father, Todd Beamer. His gift to us, his supreme act of courage, that he united in prayer before he surrendered his life together with others.[2]

How we live out our faith is the measure that calls others to live and love as Christ loved us. It challenges and gives us courage *to stand fast ... girded in truth clothed with righteousness as a breastplate ... (holding) faith as a shield, to quench all (the) flaming arrows of the evil one. And (to) take on the helmet of salvation and the sword of the Spirit, which is the word of God* (Eph 6:14, 16, 17).

A Reading

Love ... is the source of all good things; it leads to heaven. He who walks in love can neither go astray nor be afraid: love guides him, protects him, and brings him to his journey's end.[3]

Psalm Response

I trusted even when I said:
"I am sorely afflicted,"
and when I said in my alarm:
"No man can be trusted?"

How can I repay the Lord
for his goodness to me?
The cup of salvation I will raise;
I will call on the Lord's name.

My vows to the Lord I will fulfill
before all his people.
O precious in the eyes of the Lord
Is the death of his faithful.

Your servant, Lord, your servant am I;
You have loosened my bonds.
A thanksgiving sacrifice I make:
I will call on the Lord's name.[4]
Amen.

        Psalm 116:10-18

The Challenge

What makes a witness for Jesus? Is there a ministry that you can develop on behalf of others in His name?

The Church is Born

Scripture

You are strangers and aliens no longer. No, you are fellow citizens of the saints and members of the household of God. You form a building, which rises on the foundation of the apostles and prophets, with Christ Jesus Himself as the capstone. Through Him the whole structure is fitted together and takes shape as a holy temple in the Lord; in Him you are being built into this temple, to become a dwelling place for God in the Spirit.[1]

Thoughts

Abba

Centuries ago, the earth stood still as in one terrible moment the line of David was preserved. In that moment in time, the Spirit triumphed; your church was born. Honed from rock, borne of you're Son's side; its wellspring of life poured forth your Son ... its capstone. And as your house of prayer grew amid your newly chosen ones, the breath of the gift of the Spirit was revealed. For within its portals, the inner beauty of your Son's mother, Mary was revealed.[2]

Though evil lurks within its courts, we know *the gates of the netherworld shall not prevail* (Matt 16:18). Its hallowed halls are forever preserved. For the church is a spiritual house of prayer. It is the living testimony of your Son's sacred love and mercy; an everlasting promise.

To this church, we your people flock to worship you our creator and we hear your call to *come to him a living stone ... chosen and precious in the sight of God ... to be built into this house of prayer* (1 Peter2: 4), to be washed within the light of your Son's glory. For we have learned, just as your Son is in you, and you are in him: it was he who prayed on our behalf that one day we *may be brought to perfection as one* (John 17:23). It was *his divine power ... bestowed on us everything that makes for life and devotion through the knowledge of him who called us by his own glory and power. For this very reason (we must) make every effort to supplement (our) faith with virtue ...* (2 Pet 1:3, 5).

To this end Abba, we implore you to help us. You see, we are so filled with our own sense of humanness, that sometimes … more times than not, we forget to center you in our lives. Yet, the reality is none of us can ever disconnect ourselves from you. For you are the root of our existence. You are that place of wonder and mystery where all things converge in "the unity of being."[3] It is there that our personhood is born anew, in love.

A Reading

This is our house of prayer, but we too, are a house of God. If we are a house of God, its construction goes on in time so that it may be dedicated at the end of time. The house in its construction involves hard work … .

What was done when this church was being built is similar to what is done when believers are built up into Christ. When they first come to believe they are like timber and stone taken from the woods and mountains. In their instruction baptism and formation they are, so to speak, shaped, leveled and smoothed by the hands of carpenters, and craftsmen. But Christians do not make a house of God until they become one in charity. The timber and stone must fit together in an orderly plan, must be joined in perfect harmony, must give each other the support as it were of love, or no one would enter the building. When you see the stone and beams of a building holding together securely … you are not afraid of its falling down in ruins.

This house is still in process of being built in the whole world: this is the promise of prophecy. When God's house was being built after the Exile, it was prophesized in words of the psalm: *sing a new song to the Lord; sing to the Lord all the earth* … For a new song implies that Our Lord speaks of a new commandment. A new song implies a new inspiration of love. To sing is the sign of love. The singer of this song is full of the warmth of God's love.

Let us then offer our thanksgiving ... to the Lord, Our God ... let us praise His goodness with our whole heart. He it was who inspired in his faithful people the will to build this house of prayer. So God, *who gives to those of good will both the desire and the accomplishment* of the things that belong to him, the one who began this work, the one who has brought it to completion?[4]

Psalm Response

Sing joyfully to the Lord, all you lands;
serve the Lord with gladness,
come before him with joyful song.
Know that the Lord is God;
he made us, his we are;
his people, the flock he tends.
Enter his gates with thanksgiving,
his courts with praise
Give thanks to him; bless his name
for he is good
the Lord, whose kindness endures forever,
and his faithfulness, to all generations
Amen
      Psalm 100

The Challenge

We are always in the process of becoming, as is our church. Write a prayer of hope on behalf of our church. Include in it your "song" of dedication to its mission, remembering that you are a "living stone" that is being built into our house of prayer.

We must stand united with our Priests, Deacons and Religious, for we are only as strong as we are one united in our mission.

The Blessed Sacrament: The Eucharist

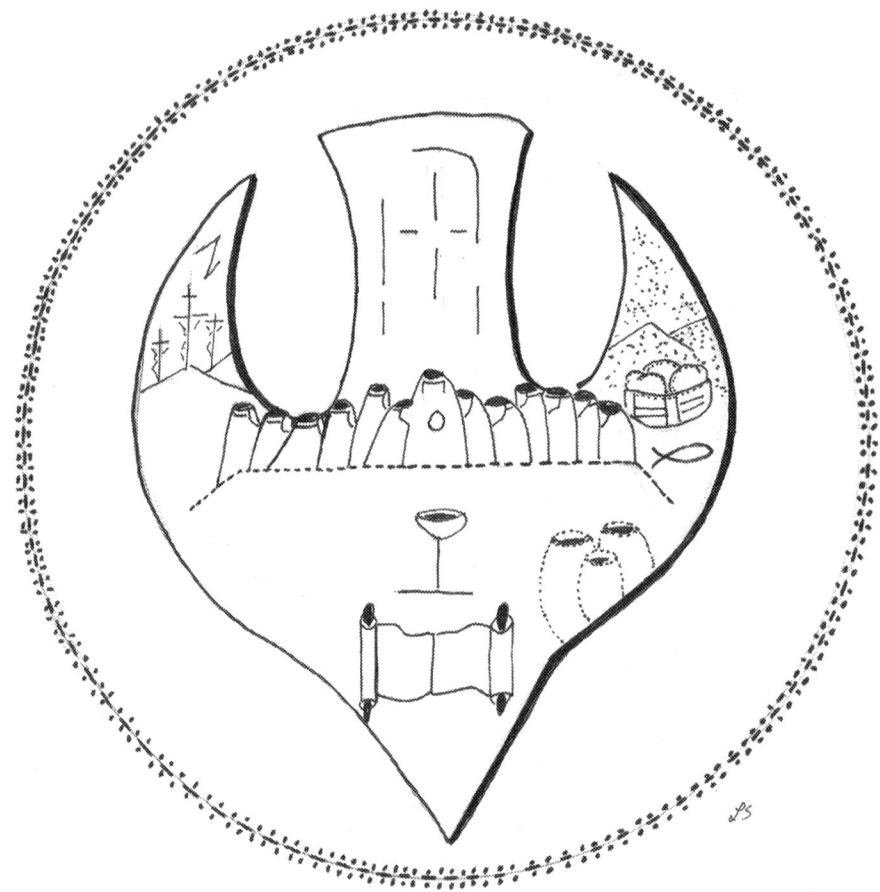

CLOCKWISE: *Manna from heaven; The miracle of the loaves; The wedding of Cana; The Last Supper; The Crucifixion; The empty Tomb.*

Scripture

While they were eating, Jesus took bread, said the blessing, broke it and giving it to his disciples said, "take and eat; this is my body." Then he took a cup, gave thanks and gave it to them saying, "Drink from it all of you, for this is my blood of the covenant, which will be shed on behalf of many for the forgiveness of sins."
      Matthew 26:26-28

Thoughts

Beloved

O Sacred Sacrament of Love
Divine Blessings from which
Life is drawn anew.

Born of a Divine encounter
That unified heaven with earth
A supreme act of love.

A gift of mercy.
A gift of charity.
A redemptive sacrifice.

The Paschal Mystery bound within the Cross
The Bread; the Body of Christ;
The Cup; His Blood.

The Risen Christ now ever-present
O Trinity
One God, Three Persons.

O Sacred Sacrament of Life.
Your blessing nourishes my soul
With faith, hope and love.

And I...
Your most humble witness
Thank you.

A Reading

He came on earth from heaven for suffering man, becoming incarnate in a virgin's womb from which he came forth as man; he took on himself the sufferings of suffering man through a body capable of suffering, and put to an end the sufferings of the flesh, and through his spirit incapable of death he became the death of death which is destructive of man.

For led like a lamb, and slaughtered like a sheep, he ransomed us from the slavery of the world of Egypt, and loosened us from the slavery of the devil as from the hand of Pharaoh, and sealed our souls with his own spirit and our bodily members with his own blood.

This is the one who covered death with the garment of reproach, who put the devil in mourning garb as Moses did Pharaoh. This is he who smote lawlessness and rendered injustice bereft of children as Moses did Egypt.

This is the one who rescued us from slavery to liberty, from darkness to light, from tyranny to the kingdom of eternity (who made us a new priesthood, a people chosen, eternal).

This is he who is the Passover of our salvation; this is he who suffered many things in many men. This is he who in Abel was slaughtered, in Jacob was exiled, in Joseph was sold, in Moses was exposed, in the lamb was immolated, in David was persecuted, in the prophets was maltreated. This is he in whom the virgin was made incarnate, on the cross was suspended, in the earth was buried, from the dead was resurrected, to the highest of heaven was lifted up.

This is the Lamb without voice, this is the lamb slaughtered, this is the lamb born of the fair ewe, this is he who was taken from the flock, and dragged to immolation, and at evening slaughtered, and by night buried.

This is he who on the cross was not broken, and in the earth did not decay, but from the dead rose again, and raised up man from the depths of the tomb.[1]

Psalm Response

O God, you are my God, for you I long
For you my soul is thirsting.
My body pines for you
Like a dry, weary land without water.
So I gaze on you in the sanctuary
to see you strength and your glory.

For your love is better than life,
my lips will speak your praise.
So I will bless you all my life.
in your name I will lift up my hands.
My soul shall be filled as with a banquet
my mouth shall praise you with joy.

On my bed I remember you.
On you I muse through the night.
For you have been my help;
in the shadow of your wings I rejoice.,
My soul clings to you;
your right hand holds me fast.
Amen.

Psalm 63:2-9[2]

The Challenge

Create a symbol, poem, song or prayer that reflects the wonder and mystery of the Eucharist. Share your creative experience with others!

The Call to Witness

Scripture

... the angel of the Lord spoke to Philip, "Get up and head south on the road that goes down from Jerusalem to Gaza, the desert route." So he got up and set out. ... Now there was an Ethiopian eunuch, a court official of the Candace, that is, the Queen of the Ethiopians, in charge of her entire treasury, who had come to Jerusalem to worship and was returning home. Seated in his chariot, he was reading the prophet Isaiah. The Spirit said to Philip, "Go and join up with that chariot." Philip ran up and heard him reading Isaiah, the prophet, and said, "Do you understand what you are reading?" He replied, "How can I, unless someone instructs me?" So he invited Philip to get in and sit with him. This was the scripture passage he was reading:

*"Like a sheep he was led to the slaughter
and as a lamb before its shearers is silent
so he opened not his mouth
In (his) humiliation justice was denied him.
Who will tell of his posterity?
For his life is taken from the earth."*

Then the eunuch said to Philip in reply, "I beg you, about whom is the prophet saying this? About himself, or about someone else?" Then Philip opened his mouth and, beginning with this scripture passage, he proclaimed Jesus to him. As they traveled along the road they came to some water and the eunuch said, "look, there is water. What is to prevent me from being baptized?" Then he ordered the chariot to stop and Philip and the eunuch both went down into the water, and he baptized him. When they came out of the water the Spirit of the Lord snatched Philip away, and the eunuch saw him no more, but continued on his way, rejoicing.
    Acts 8:26-39

Thoughts

Beloved Jesus

A disciple is born of an inward well that yearns for the living God. The fountain of water overflows. It is to you we sing praise. It is to you we give thanks. Blessed are those who believe.

A Reading

> O Crystal well!
> O that on your silvered surface
> You would mirror forth at once
> Though eyes I have desired.
> Which I bear sketched deep within my heart
>
> Faith is called crystal for two reasons: because it is of Christ the Bridegroom and because it has the property of crystal, pure in its truth, a limped well without error or natural forms in it.
>
> It is a well because the waters of spiritual goodness flow from it to the soul. Christ our Lord speaking to the Samaritan woman calls faith a well, saying: "The water that I shall give him will become in him a well of water springing up to eternal life." This water is the Spirit, which those who believe receive through faith in him.
>
> I know the fountain well which flows and runs through the night.
> That everlasting fountain is a secret well,
> And I know well its home
> Though of the night
> I know that nothing that can be in beauty like it.
> And that of it heaven and earth do drink
> Though of the night.[1]

Psalm Response

I will extol you, O my God and King,
and I will bless your name forever and ever.
Every day will I bless you
and I will praise your name for ever and ever.
Amen
     Psalm 145 1-2

The Challenge

Think about a time that God has personally helped you. The next time you meet someone who shares they have a problem, listen to their concerns. Then share with them how God helped you. In that very moment you are for The Beloved, His Witness!

Who Do You Say I Am?

Scripture

"... when I go to the Israelites and say to them, 'The God of your fathers has sent me to you,' if they ask me, 'What is his name?' what am I to tell them?" God replied, "I am who am." Then he added "This is what you shall tell the Israelites: I Am sent me to you."
   Exodus 3:13-14

When Jesus went into the region of Caesarea Philippi he asked his disciples, "Who do people say that the Son of Man is?" They replied, "Some say John the Baptist, others Elijah, still others Jeremiah or one of the prophets." He said to them, "But who do you say that I am?" Simon Peter said in reply, "You are the Messiah, the Son of the Living God." Jesus said to him in reply "Blessed are you, Simon, son of Jonah. For flesh and blood has not revealed this to you, but my heavenly Father."
   Matthew 16: 13-17

Thoughts

My Lord

Within your name are hidden gifts, the essence of your presence. You are The Living Faith, The Hidden One who entreats one's soul to enter your fold. You are our Wonder-Counselor, the Healer and our Shepherd who guides us along paths never traveled before. You, my Lord, are my Triune God; The Father, The Son and the Holy Spirit; my Redeemer. You are the Risen Christ, my Savior. The One I call my Beloved; the One I know as Love. The One who lives in the deepest recess of my soul. Who do you say I Am? You, My Lord are the heart of our bleeding world.

A Reading

Our Father most holy, our Creator, Our Redeemer, Our Savior, our Consoler.

Who art in heaven, in the angels and in the saints: you

enlightened them that they may know you, because you, Lord, are the Light; you make them burn that they may love you, because you, Lord, are love; you dwell in them and fill them that they may possess all happiness, because you, Lord, are the Supreme good, the eternal good, from which comes every good, and outside of whom no good exists.

Hallowed be the name: that we may know you clearly so as to comprehend the breadth of your gifts, the extent of your promises, the height of your majesty, the depths of your judgments.

Thy kingdom come: so that you may reign in us with your grace and enable us to reach your kingdom, where we shall see you with our love for you made perfect, in blessed companionship with you, enjoying you eternally.

Thy will be done on earth as it is in heaven. Grant that we may love you with all our heart, thinking of you without ceasing; with all our soul, desiring you always; with all our mind directing every intention toward you and seeking your glory in everything; with all our strength, using every energy and power of our soul and body in the service of your love alone.[1]

Psalm Response

"Even the Sparrow finds a home,
and the Swallow a nest
in which she puts her young –
Your altars, O Lord of Hosts,
my King and my God!"
Amen.
     Ps. 84: 4

The Challenge

Who Do You Say I Am?

Part Three:
The Call to Prayer

"... ask and you will receive; seek and you will find; knock and the door will be opened to you."
Luke 11:9

God is Listening

Scripture

... if my people upon whom my name has been pronounced, humble themselves and pray and seek my presence and turn from their evil ways, I will hear them from heaven ... and pardon their sense and revive their land. Now my eyes shall be open and my ears attentive to the prayer of this place.
    2 Chronicles 7, 14

Is anyone among you suffering? He should pray. Is anyone in good spirits? He should sing praise. Is anyone among you sick? He should summon the presbyters of the church, and they should pray over him and anoint (him) with oil in the name of the Lord and the prayer of faith will save the sick person and the Lord will raise him up. If he has committed any sins he will be forgiven. The fervent prayer of a righteous person is very powerful.
    James 5:15

... do not cease praying ... and asking that you may be filled with the knowledge of his will through all spiritual wisdom and understanding to live in a manner worthy of the Lord, so as to be fully pleasing, in every good work bearing fruit and growing in the knowledge of God, strengthened with every power, in accord with his glorious might. For all endurance and patience, with joy giving thanks to the Father, who has made you fit to share in the inheritance of the holy ones in light. He delivered us from the power of darkness and transferred us to the kingdom of his beloved Son, in whom we have redemption, the forgiveness of sins.
    Colossians 1:5-13

Thoughts

To the Reader

Pray for the gift of faith. It carries the power of love. Pray to believe. To trust in He who is Love. Pray for the light of life. He is yours forever and ever.

A Reading

How great is the good, which God works in a soul when he gives it a disposition to pray in earnest. If that soul perseveres in spite of sins, temptations and relapses, brought about in a thousand ways by Satan, our Lord will bring it at last—I am certain of it—to the harbor of salvation … .

He who gives himself to prayer is in possession of a great blessing. Let him never cease from prayer who has once begun it, be his life ever so wicked; for prayer is the way to amend it.

As for him who has not begun to pray, I implore him by the love of our Lord not to deprive himself of so great a good.[1]

Psalm Response

Glorify the Lord with me
let us together extol his name.
I sought the Lord and he answered me
and delivered me from all my fears.
Look to him, that you may be radiant
with joy.
Amen.
           Psalm 34: 4-6

The Challenge

If God is always ready to listen to our pleas, why is it so difficult to remember to pray? Could it be that we are short on faith?

What is God Asking of You?

Scripture

With what shall I come before the Lord,
and bow before God most high?
Shall I come before him with holocausts,
with calves a year old?
Will the Lord be pleased
with thousands of rams with myriad streams of oil?
Shall I give my first-born for my crime,
the fruit of my body for the sin of my soul?
You have been told, O man, what is good,
and what the Lord requires of you:
Only to do right and to love goodness
and to walk humbly with your God.
     Micah 6:6-8

Thoughts

Beloved Jesus

If one lives life centered in you, our actions can become another's blessing. Kindness grows within the heart. Loving you is to profoundly know you're never-ending mercy and forgiveness. To love you, is to walk with you forever, humbled by your ever-lasting compassion.

A Reading

Anyone who really loves God loves everything good,
wants everything good, stands up for everything good,
praises everything good, always sides with good people and
supports them and defends them. People like this only love
what is genuine and things that deserve to be loved.[1]

Psalm Response

O Lord, our Lord
how glorious is your name over all the earth!
You have exalted your majesty above the heavens
Out of the mouth of babes and sucklings
you have fashioned praise because of your foes,
to silence the hostile and the vengeful.
When I behold your heavens, the work of your fingers,
the moon and the stars which you sit in place.
What is man that you should be mindful of him...

You have made him little less than the angels
and crowned him with glory and honor.
You have given him rule over the works of your hands,
putting all things under his feet.
All sheep and oxen, yes, and the beasts of the field,
The birds of the air, the fishes of the sea,
And whatever swims the path of the seas.
O Lord, our Lord how glorious is your name
over all the earth!
Amen.
      Psalm 8

The Challenge

Have you ever considered that little acts of love on behalf of others can become ... blessings?

Think about an experience where you voluntarily helped another simply out of love? Then remember to thank Jesus. You see, the blessing is also yours!

In Darkness There is Light

SCRIPTURE

For you darkness itself is not dark,
and night shines as day.
(Darkness and light) are the same.
    Psalm 139:12

THOUGHTS

Beloved Jesus

It is in the depth of darkness that one's soul struggles to find you. It moves here and there, covering long distances until it looses itself in a wave of perfect stillness. Comforted by this quiet recess in time, the soul finally learns to surrender its will. And, when it stirs, finds it is embraced within your never-ending circle of love. Dawn is here.

A READING

Live in faith and hope even though you are in darkness, for in this darkness God enfolds the soul. Cast your cares upon God, for you are his, and he will never forget you.[1]

PSALM RESPONSE

I will give thanks to you, O Lord with all my heart
(for you have heard the words of my mouth)
in the presence of the angels I will sing your praise;
I will worship at your holy temple
and give thanks to your name,
Because of your kindness and your truth;
for you have made great above all things
your name and your promise.
Amen.
    Psalm 138:1-2

The Challenge

Have you ever experienced a time of darkness in your prayer life? It is not unusual, but it can be difficult. Why not discuss it with a spiritual director?

Rachel's Children

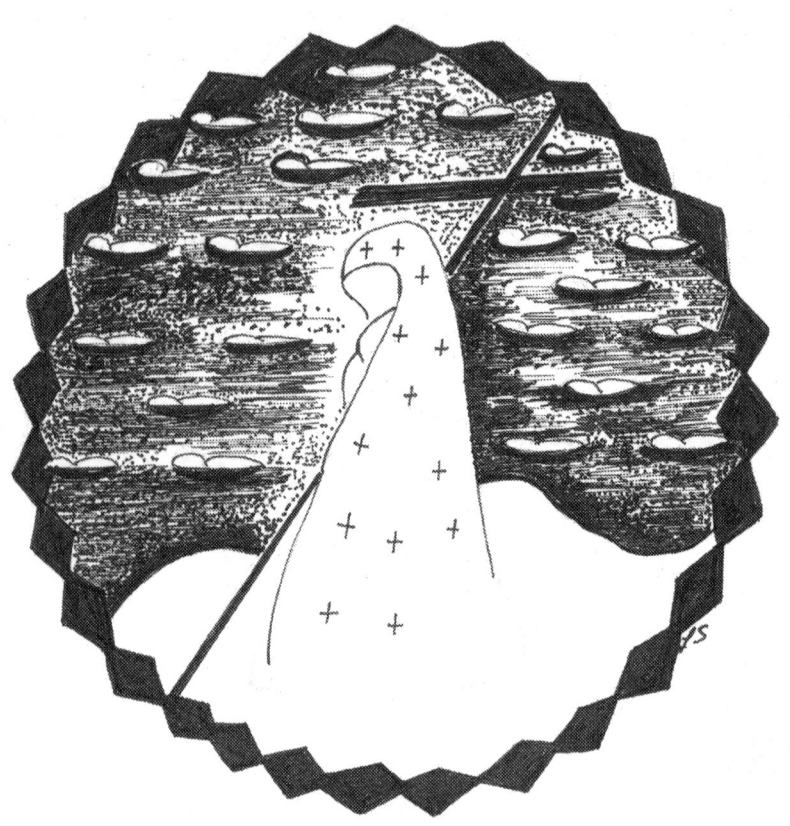

SCRIPTURE

A voice was heard in Ramah sobbing and loud lamentation, Rachel weeping for her children and she would not be consoled since they were no more.
    Matthew 2:18

THOUGHTS

Beating hearts extinguished
And with each we lose
a certain sense of our humanity.
Father forgive us!

A READING

I can not disconnect myself from my God.
He is the being of my being, the root of my root
and all things converge on the unity of being.
And hence, a woman's womb with a child in it
is the best simile we have for
the relationship between God and man. ...[1]

PSALM RESPONSE

*Behold you are pleased with sincerity of heart
and in my inmost being you teach me wisdom.
Cleanse me of sin with hyssop, that I may be purified;
wash me, and I shall be whiter than snow.
A clean heart create for me O God,
and a steadfast spirit renew within me.
Cast me not out from your presence...
My sacrifice, O God, is a contrite spirit; a heart contrite and humbled...
O God, you will not spurn.
Amen.*
    Psalm 51: 8 ,9,12,13,19

The Challenge

Pray for life!

In Celebration of a Life:
St. Teresa Benedicta of the Cross

Scripture

... Let him who is thirsty come forward; let all who desire it accept the gift of life-giving water.
        Revelation 22:17

Thoughts

Beloved Jesus

So it was that Edith Stein, a woman of the 20th century, a daughter of Abraham, phenomenologist, and seeker of truth became a Catholic convert from Judaism: a Carmelite Nun and Saint. Edith Stein asked for truth; found you our living Messiah and traveled the way of the cross until she became enfolded in its blessing.[1] Edith Stein, a woman of prayer, understood that if one's soul was to be in union with you, it would have to be "purchased through the cross; consummated on the cross and sealed for all eternity with the sign of the cross."[2] As the world around her became engulfed in Nazi terrorism, this woman of prayer wrote a letter to the Superior of her convent, requesting she be permitted to center her life of prayer as a "victim of atonement for the peace of the world."[3] Edith Stein never forgot her roots. She never forgot her people. She was a believer, a woman of the cross. Three years later in 1942, this Carmelite Nun was confined and died in the concentration camp at Auschwitz. Edith Stein walked the way of the Cross and endured the suffering of the cross. She knocked, the door opened and she was swept into your divine light for all eternity.

A Reading

> ... there came a day when, through all creation
> there occurred a fissure. All the elements seemed
> To be in revolt, night enveloped
> The world at noon. But in the midst of the night
> There stood as if illumined by lightening a barren mountain.
> And on the mountain a cross on which someone hung

Bleeding from a thousand wounds; a thirst came over us
To drink ourselves well from this fountain of wounds.
The cross vanished into night, yet our night
Was suddenly penetrated by a new light
Of which we had never had any idea: a sweet blessed light
It streamed from the wounds of that man
Who had just died on the cross; now he stood
In our midst. He himself was the light,
The eternal light, that we have longed for from old,
The Father's reflection and the salvation of the people,
He spread his arms wide and spoke
With a voice full of heavenly timbre:
Come to me all you who have faithfully served
The Father and lived in hope
Of the redeemer; see, he is with you,
He fetches you home to his Father's kingdom.
What happened then, there are no words to describe,
All of us who had awaited blessedness,
We were now at our goal- in the heart of Jesus.[4]

Psalm Response

Only a breath are mortal men;
an illusion are men of rank;
In balance they prove lighter.
all together, than a breath.
One thing God said: these two things
Which I heard;
that power belongs to God, and
yours, O Lord, is kindness
and that you render to everyone
according to his deeds.
Amen.
      Psalm 62:10, 12

The Challenge

Read about the life of Edith Stein. Discuss her life with others.

Develop a prayer that reflects her life, your needs and those of our world.

The Tree of Life

Scripture

Then the angel showed me the river of life-giving water, sparkling like crystal, flowing from the throne of God and of the Lamb down the middle of its street. On either side of the river grew the tree of life that produces fruit twelve times a year, once every month; the leaves of the trees serve as medicine for the nations. Nothing accursed will be found there anymore. The throne of God and of the Lamb will be it and his servants will worship him. They will look upon his face and his name will be on their foreheads. Night will be no more, nor will they need light from lamp or sun, for the Lord God shall give them light, and they shall reign forever and ever.
    Revelation 22:1-5

Thoughts

Abba

As The Tree of Life is nourished by waters that *flow from your sanctuary*, we beseech you, O Lord, to come to our aid (Ezek 47:12). Our world is in need of awareness that will expand our understanding of the impact of culture and religion on one's identity. Help us see clearly the different dimensions of the problem. Humanity is rich in its diversity. Indeed, difference was always a part of your Divine Plan.[1] For we wear a coat of many colors and patterns. Yet, history has a way of reliving its past. Division in this postmodern world has widened. Waves of global terrorism abound, soaked in the blood of ancient disputes. At the same time, the magnitude of streams of abject poverty and disease is so great that it confronts the senses. Secularism is riding high on the back of technology in its own quest for freedom that is misunderstood. Help us recognize that only within your presence can one find the mystical balm that brings peace. Why is it so difficult for us to realize, hope with its transforming power exits where there is Love?

A Reading

Human beings were not created to be strangers to one another, to ignore one another externally, but rather to be companions to one another, brothers and sisters who love and help one another and gather together around their Father who provides for their daily needs. ... From him each one receives the same blessing and all are heading for the same destination, their Father's house.[2]

Psalm Response

It is good to give thanks to the Lord
to sing praise to your name, Most High,
To proclaim your kindness at dawn
and your faithfulness throughout the night,
With ten-stringed instrument and Lyre,
with melody upon the harp.
For you make me glad, O Lord, by your deeds;
at the works of your hands, I rejoice.

How great are your works, O Lord!
How very deep are your thoughts!
A senseless man knows not,
nor does a fool understand this
Though the wicked flourish like grass
and all evildoers thrive,
They are destined for eternal destruction;
while you O Lord, are the Most High forever.

The just man shall flourish like the palm tree,
like a cedar of Lebanon shall he grow.
They that are planted in the house
of the Lord shall flourish in the courts of our God.
They shall bear fruit even in old age;
vigorous and sturdy shall they be.

Declaring how just is the Lord
my Rock, in whom there is no wrong.
Amen.
        Psalm 92:1-9, 13-16

The Challenge

What can we do to expand our understanding of culture and its impact on one's religious identity?

How can we reach out in friendship to others? Develop a plan and share it.

Pray and remember to thank God for His help.

Epilogue

"I have called you by name. You are mine. You are my witnesses," says the Lord, "my servants whom I have chosen. To know and believe in me and understand that it is I ... I am the Lord, your Holy One ... ."
  Isaiah 43:1,10,15

To The Reader:

To be called by God is an invitation to Love; to hear, without hearing; to see, without seeing; yet knowing from a place somewhere deep inside, that you are indeed loved by Him. To be called by God is to open one's heart and breathe in life anew and then to simply follow Him through Life. Our Lord's call is one of wonder and mystery. It is all that is profound and more times than not, defies comprehension. It is a gift of faith.

Praying is an essential part of that gift. It is our opportunity to be present to Him. Scripture is an entry point. My prayer for you is that the Holy Spirit will grace your journey with many moments with the Sacred.

Endings are simply new beginnings. This is now your time to find in scripture your own inspirational texts and readings. It is your time for private devotion, a time to be filled with creative expression. It is a time to find a personal ministry, to witness your Christian faith, believing in Christ's transforming power and knowing that as you step forward, you are accepting His call.

This is your time to seek. It is your moment to begin ... to live life!

Glossary of Terms and Sources

Dei Verbum
Dogmatic Constitution on Divine Revelation
Pope Paul VI
1965
The Old and New Testaments

"The principle purpose to which the plan of the covenant was directed was to prepare for the coming of Christ, the redeemer of all and of the messianic kingdom, to announce this coming by prophecy and to indicate its meanings... Now the books of the Old Testament, reveal to all me the knowledge of God and of man and the ways in which God just and merciful deals with men. These books contain a store of sublime teachings about God sound wisdom about human life and a wonderful treasury of prayer and in them the mystery of our salvation is present in a hidden way, God the inspirer and author of both Testaments wisely arranged that the New Testament be hidden in the Old and the Old be made manifest in the New. For though Christ established the new covenant in His blood... the books of the Old Testament with all their parts caught up into the proclamation of the Gospel, acquire and show forth their full meaning in the New Testament and in turn shed light on it and explain it."

Lumen Gentuim
Dogmatic Constitution On The Church
Pope Paul VI
1964
Laity:

"The term laity is here understood to mean all the faithful. What specifically characterizes the laity is their secular nature. By their very vocation (they) seek the kingdom of God by engaging in temporal affairs and by offering them according to the plan of God. They live in the world; that is, in each and all of the secular professions and occupations. They live in the ordinary circumstances of family and social life from which the very web of their existence is woven;. They are called there by God that by experiencing their proper function and led by the spirit of the Gospel they may work for the Sanctification of the world from within as a leaven. In this way they may make Christ known to others, especially by the testimony of a life resplendent in faith, hope and charity."

The laity are gathered together in the People of God and make up the Body of Christ under one head. Whoever they are they are called upon as living members to expend all their energy for the growth of the Church and its continuous sanctification since this very energy is a gift of the Creator and Blessing of the Redeemer.

The lay apostolate, however, is a participation in the Salvific mission of the Church itself. Through their baptism and confirmation all are commissioned to that apostolate by the Lord Himself. Moreover, by the sacraments, especially holy Eucharist, that charity toward God and man, which is the soul of the apostolate, is communicated and nourished. Now the laity are called in a special way to make the Church present and operative in those places and circumstances where only through them can it become the salt of the earth. Thus every layman, in virtue of the very gifts bestowed upon him is at the same time a witness and a living instrument of the mission of the church itself" according to the measure of Christ's bestowal". Upon all the laity therefore, rests the noble duty of working to extend the divine plan of salvation to all men of each epoch and in every land.

The National Cursillo Center
Dallas Texas
www.natl-cursillo.org
The Cursillo Movement:

Cursillo is a world-wide movement. It originated in Spain during the 1940s and seeks to find ways to bring the Church to life in the heart of the Laity. In the Cursillo Movement evangelization is approached as a natural act of being Christ like within our daily activities. Its purpose is to bring about apostolic change in our society, church and the world with the membership at large agents of change within their families, work situations neighborhoods and social gathering. In 1980 The Cursillo Movement received the apostolic blessing of divine grace by Pope John Paul II.

Mental Prayer
St. Theresa of Avila

"Whoever has not begun the practice of prayer, I beg for the love of the Lord not to go without so great a good. There is nothing here to fear but only to desire. Even if there be no great progress, or much effort in reaching such perfection as to deserve the favors and mercies God bestows on the more generous, at least a person will come to understand the read leading to heaven. And if one perseveres, I trust then in the mercy of God, who never fails to repay anyone who has taken Him for a friend. For mental prayer in my opinion is nothing else than an intimate sharing between friends; it means taking time frequently to be alone with Him whom we know loves us."

Kiean, Kavanaugh, OCD, Otilio, Rodriguez, OCD translators. *The Collected Works of St. Theresa of Avila.* Vol. 1 (Washington D.C. ICB Publications. Institute of Carmelite Studies, 1987). p. 44

Lectio Divina

Letting our Divine Friend speak to us through his inspired and inspiring Word. It includes our response to that Word, to his communication to us through that Word. Lectio is meeting with a friend, a very special Friend who is God; listening to him, really listening and responding, in intimate prayer and in the way we take that Word and let it shape our lives.

The Method of Lectio:
1. Take the Sacred Text with reverence and call upon the Holy Spirit
2. For ten minutes (or longer, if you are so drawn), listen to the Lord speaking to you through the Text and respond to him
3. At the end of the time, choose a word or phrase (perhaps one will have been "given " to you to take with you, and thank the Lord for being with you and speaking to you.

M. Basil Pennington O C SO Lectio Divina Renewing the Ancient Practice of Praying the Scriptures (New York: Crossroad Book Publishing Co. 1998) pxi, p. 151.

Collective Memory

Although each of us has a unique set of memories, we also have shared memories of our historical record and our collective achievements and mistakes. The expansion of this shared consciousness through the promotion of learning can help to guide us towards a more ethical future in which previous human and environmental tragedies are not perpetuated. ...

www.google.com/search?hl=en&q=define+collective+memory&btnG=Search

END NOTES

INTRODUCTION

1. See Glossary
2. This truth was explained to me by Sister Christine O'Brien, OCD Carmelite Monastery, Elysburg, Pa.
3. M. Basil Pennington OCD, *Lectio Devina: Renewing the Ancient Practice of Praying the Scriptures* (New York: Crossroad 1998) p. xi.
4. Cardinal Joseph Ratzinger. "The Sign of The Woman An Introduction to the Encyclical "Redemptoris Mater" *Mary: God's Yes to Man John Paul's, Encyclical Redemptoris Mater* (San Francisco: Ignatius Pres, 1987) p. 11.
5. Daniel J. Harrington S J, "How To Get The Most Out of Reading The Bible. *U S Catholic* (October, 1998) p. 18.

ABRAHAM SARAH AND HAGAR

1. Thoughts about our collective memory were inspired by several articles found on the web. They are as follows: **A.** Henry Abramson "Collective Memory and Collective Identity": Jews, Rusyn and the Holocaust, Carpatho-Rusyn, American Fall. 1994. Vol XVII no. 3; **B.** Revenge of a child. Uri Avnery. **C.** The Meaning of Home Arjan El Fossed; **D.** For A Sociology Of Collective Memory Marie-Claire Lavabre; **E.** Tramautic Places of Collective Memory Liliana Ddeyanova (Bulgarian History).
2. Ted Szule "Abraham Father of Three Faiths" Journal of The National Geographic Society (December 2001: p. 128. 3. Anselm Gruim, *Images of Jesus The Jesus who Weeps* Trans. John Bacoden New York (Contiuum2002) p. 101.
4. L. Gelber and Michael Linssen OCD, ed., Waltraut Stein Phd trans., *The Hidden Life Hagiographic Essays Meditations Spiritual Texts* (Washington DC ICS Publications Institute of Carmelite Studies 1992) p. 133.

THE TESTING OF ABRAHAM

1. Xavier Leon-Defour ed., *Dictionary of Biblical Theology*. (New York, Seabury Press, 1973) p. 4.
2. Ibid 4. Abraham was living in the land of Canaan where infant sacrifice

was being practiced at that time.
3. Origin, Priest, from a homily, on Genesis (homily 86, 89: pp. 202-209) *The Divine Office of the Liturgy of the Hours* 11 (New York), Catholic Book Publishing Co. 1975) p. 180.
4. Charles de Foucald, *"Meditation" Divine Intimacy* 11 Gabriel of St. Mary Magdelene, OCD (San Fransisco, Ignatius Press 1987) p. 32.

THE CALL OF MOSES

1. Bernhard Anderson, *Understanding the Old Testament* (Englewood Cliffs, New Jersey, Prentice Hall Inc. 1975) p. 52.
2. Joseph Telushkin, Rabbi *Jewish Literacy* (William Morrow and Company, Inc. New York 1991) p. 47.
3. Monika Helwig, *Understanding Catholicism* (New York, Paulist Press 1981 pp. 15,17, 18, 20. My primary thoughts for this meditation were inspired by this writing.
4. Gloria Durka, *Praying with Hildegard of Bingen* (Winona Minnesota, St Mary's Press Christian Brothers Publications, 1991) p. 101.

THE EXODUS

1. The Central Conference of American Rabbis Ed., *The Union Haggadah: Home Service for the Passover* (USA 1923) p. 38.
2. Ibid. Isaac Mayer Wise, "Freedom" Sermons by American Rabbis, 1896 p. 181, 152.
3. Saint John Chrysostom, bishop "Christ and Moses (Cat. 3, 24-27: Sc50, 165-167) *The Divine Liturgy of The Hours* 11 op cit., p. 160, 161.

THE TEN COMMANDMENTS

1. Father Gabriel of St Magdalene OCD 11 op. cit., pp. 57, 58.

THE RATIFICATION OF THE COVENANT

1. Thoughts were inspired by Leviticus 17:11. 3 Pope John II Veritas Splenda Origins, CNS Documentary Services 23 No 18 Oct 14 1993.
2. Raymond E. Brown Ss, Joseph A. Fitzmeyer, SJ, E. O. Roland, O Carm Ed. *The New Jerome Handbook* (Liturgical Press 1992) p. 403.

3. *The New American Bible* p. 96. See textural notes "blood was from an ox, sheep ... ."
4. In February 2006 Sister Angela Prioress of the Carmelite Monastery, Elysburg, Pa. discussed the above scripture passages as well as her thoughts, which I included in the paragraph. These conversations, as well as, many others were special gifts to be treasured.
5. The Divine Liturgy of the Hours 11 op cit., p. 286-288. I strongly urge reading this homily on Leviticus by Origen, priest.
6. John Nelson. *The Little Way of Saint Therese of Liseux*, (Ligori, Missouri: Ligori Press 1997) p. 121-122.

The Book of Ruth

1. Katherine Spint, Ed. *Life in the Spirit: Reflections, Meditations, Prayers. Mother Teresa of Calcutta.* Harper and Row (San Francisco, Harper and Row, 1983) p. 33.

Solomon's Judgment

1. Saint Catherine of Sienna, *I Tasted and I Saw* From a dialogue on Divine Providence (cap. 167, Gra tiarun actio ad Trinitarium: ed. Lat., Ingo/stadii 1583 f. 290 v-29, *The Divine Office of the Liturgy Of the Hours* 11 op cit., p. 1795.

Out of The Whirlwind

1. Christian Bible. Translated, Presented and Commented for the Christian Communities of the Phillippines and the Third World and For Those Who Seek God (Quezon City, Clariton Pulications, 1988) p. 766, see Footnotes.
2. Dorothy Sole, "Suffering From a Feminist Perspective" Lucien, Richard, OMI. *Human Suffering: What Are They Saying About The Theology Of Suffering.* (New York: Paulist Press.1992) p. 86.
3. *The New Jerome Bible Handbook* op.cit p. 156.
4. Elie Wiesel, "The Solitude of God" *Walking With God In A Fragile World,* James Langford and Leroy S Rouner, Ed. (New York: Rowman and Littlefield, Inc 2003) p. 90.

THE STORY OF TOBIT

1. William A. Barry, SJ Paying *Attention to God: Discernment In Prayer* (Indiana, Ave Maria Press, 1973) pp. 49-51. I found these thoughts to be quite interesting.
2. Venerable Louis of Grenada, "What Martha Learned" Magnificat 7. No. 5 (July 21 2005) pp. 398, 399.

THE BOOK OF ESTHER

1. *Christian Community Bible* op, cit., p. 844, footnotes.
2. Joseph Telushkin, Rabbi, op cit., pp. 107, 108.
3. The New American Bible op. cit., See introduction, The Book of Esther, p. 460. Note information regarding the differences in the original Hebrew text; i.e., omission of references to God and of His Providence over Israel. Note the contrast in the later Greek text, which I chose to use for this meditation.
4. Pierre Teilhard de Chardin. *The Divine Milieu: An Essay on The Interior Life*. (New York: Harper and Rowe 1960) p. 51.

MARY MOTHER OF GOD

1. Pope John Paul II: Mary: God's Yes to Man., Encyclical Letter, Mother of The Redeemer (San Francisco: Ignatius Press) 1988 p. 2.

THE VISITATION

1. Robert J. Morneau. *Fathoming Bethlehem, Advent Meditations*. New York: Crossroad, 1997) p. 64.
2. *Divine Intimacy 11* op. cit., 11 pp. 202, 205. Mary Catherine Nolan, OP *Mary's Song Living Her Timeless Prayer* (Notre Dame, Indiana Ave Maria Press 2001) p. 126. This is a lovely book. The Chapter "Holy is God's Name was particularly inspiring.
3. Morneau, op cit., pp. 64-65.
4. This psalm was taken from the Carmelite Proper of The Hours of The Order Of The Brothers Of The Blessed Virgin Mary Of Mount Carmel and of The Order of Discalced Carmelites Rome Institutuna Carmelitaneum 1993 p. 289. The text of this psalm is from The Grail translation.

The Presentation

1. *Divine Intimacy* 1. Op. Cit. pp. 275, 276. This reflection once again was inspired after reading Father Gabriel. His four volumes are magnificent! It is no wonder I chose a format that is similar to his.
2. Ibid. p. 277.

The Holy Family

1. Jose Luis Gonzalez- Belado Comp, *Mother Teresa: In My Own Words.* (New York: Gramercy Books 1996) p. 47.

The Baptism of Jesus

1. Elizabeth of the Trinity OCD *I Have Found God* Complete Works Vol. 1, Aletheia Kane OCD (Washington Province of Discalced Carmelites, Inc. ICS Publications 1984) p. 105.

A Lesson From The Beloved

1. Vanier Jean. "*Getting Real with Jesus*" Magnificat August 2001 Vol 3 No. 6 p. 59.

The Call to Faith

1. Both the symbolic scripture image and thoughts were inspired after reading the article An Eagle Soars at Easter: The Gospel of John by Ronald D Witherup, SS, in Saint Anthony Messenger April 2004 Volume111 Number 11 pp. 13-17.
2. Ciszek, Walter J S.J. and Flattery, Daniel SJ *He Leadeth Me* (New York: Doubleday, 1973) p. 32.

The Transfiguration

1. Anastasues of Sinai, Bishop. "It is Good For Us to Be Here" From a sermon on the Transfiguration The Liturgy of The Hours 1V Ordinary Time Weeks 18-34 op. cit., p. 1286.
2. Dictionary of Biblical Theology, op. cit., pp. 610, 611.

3. Pope John Paul II Apostolic Letter Rosaruim Virginis Mareal http:/www.Vatican.va.Holy-Father/John-Paul-II/apost-letters/documents/hf-jp-ii-apl-2002 p. 5.
4. Pope John Paul II and Messori Vittorio. Ed Crossing *The Threshold of Hope*. (New York: Alfred A. Knoff 1994) pp.194, 195.
5. Demetrius Dumm O.S.B. *Praying The Scriptures*. (Collegeville Minnesota: Liturgical Press, 2003) p. 73.
6. This psalm was taken from the Liturgy Of The Hours. Vol. III p. 592.

THE AGONY IN THE GARDEN

1. Karl Rahner, SJ *The Practice of Faith, Love and Hope*. (New York: Crossroad 1984) pp. 82-85, 94.
2. *Understanding the Old Testament* op. cit., p. 365. These words were inspired first by reading Habakkuk and then tracing its significance. Note Anderson's statement: "The prophet takes his stand on his 'watchtower of faith' to await Yahweh's answer. But no immediate answer is given. The answer that comes is when he [2; 1-5] 'lifts his eyes to the horizon of the future when God's purpose ultimately would be realized.'"
3. loc. cit., Karl Rahner.
4. Koeller, Marie Noel RSM April 27, 2002 Scripture Seminar at Miserecordia This seminar provided an opportunity for additional meditation on The Agony in The Garden.
5. Sr. Mary ODC, ed. *Daily Readings with St. Teresa of Avila* (*Springfield, Illinois* Templegate. 1983. p. 36.

THE WAY OF THE CROSS

1 .Karl.Rahner, op. cit., pp. 145-148.
2. Jean Babtiste SJ: Blessed Claude De La Columbure, SJ Trustful Surrender To Divine Providence, Rockford, Illinois, Tan Books 1961. p. 39.
3. Gabriel of St. Mary Magdalen, OCD, *Divine Intimacy*, ll, op cit., p. 56.
4. Librerea Editrice Vaticana Catechism of The Catholic Church. United States Conference 1994 (598) see notation (392) St. Francis of Assisi, Admonitions 5, 3 .
5. Ibid. 597.
6. Ibid. 598.

7. These words are printed on the back of each cross-given at the formal ceremony of introduction to Cursillo.
8. Dagobert D. Runes. *Dictionary of Philosophy* (Maryland Littlefield, Adams Quality Paperbooks, 1983) p. 285.
9. These words were taken from Psalm 46 Liturgy of the Hours Vol 3 p. 804.
10. Ibid p. 803.
11. Saint Gregory The Great Pope: "The Mystery of our New Life in Christ" (lib.13.21-23: PL75-1028-1029) The Divine Office of The Liturgy of The Hours ll op. cit. pp. 257-259.
12. I utilized the following narratives, meditations, commentaries and scripture for my personal prayer and meditation on the Stations of the Cross during lent 2005. I would recommend their use to others interested in the Lectio Divino method of prayer:
Binz, Steven J. *The Passion and Ressurection Narratives of Jesus.* A commentary. The Liturgical Press, Collegeville Minn. 1955 p. 126. *The Way Of The Cross,* Barton Cotton, Inc. Baltimore, Md. 1965 *The Way Of The Cross Meditations of Pope John Paul II,* The Catholic Nearest Welfare Association, New York, NY 1962 Henri J.M. Nouwen. *Way Of The Cross Meditations.* Communications for the Parish. 1990.

THE EMPTY TOMB

1. These are words spoken at the Easter Vigil Mass. Father Al Sceski, Christ the King Church Benton, Pa. 2004.
2. Karl Rahner S J op. cit., p. 67.
3. Chesterton G. K. *The Everlasting Man* (San Francisco Ignatius Press, 1999) p. 213.

THE MARTYRDOM OF ST STEPHEN

1. Strassner, Henry E, Rev. Church of St Jerome, Tamaqua, Pa. Homily on Jan 1 2003.
2. Beamer Lisa, Ken Abraham, Lets *Roll* Tyndale House Publishers 2002.
3. The Divine Office of the Liturgy of The Hours 1 op. cit., 1257.
4. Ibid. 1417.

The Church is Born

1. The Divine Office of The Liturgy of The Hours.ll Op cit. p1881. I elected to use the scripture text from the Office.
2. George A Maloney S J , Mary: The Womb of God Albrisi Press, p. 11
3. Carlos Coretto, Robert Barr Trans, I *Sought and I Found* (Maryknoll, New York : Orbis Books 1983) p. 82, 83.
4. Saint Augustine, bishop (Sermon 336,1.6: PL 38 (edit.1861), 1471-1472.1475) Liturgy of the Hours ll op cit., p 1894, 1895.

The Blessed Sacrament

1. Daniel P Guernsey Comp. *Adoration: Eucharistic Texts and Prayers Throughout Church History* (San Fransico Ignatius Press 1999) Pages 34,35
2. The Office of the Blessed Sacrament Nocturnal Adoration Society New York1992. The Grail Edition of the Psalms was used A. P. Watt and Son of London " David wrote this Psalm when he was in the desert, and longed to see God in His sanctuary. All night long we use his words to express our desire to love and serve God." p. 69.

The Call to Witness

1. Sister Elizabeth Ruth OCD. Ed. *Daily Readings with St John of the Cross*. (Springfield, Illinois. Templegate 1985) p. 73.

Who Do You Say I Am

1. St. Francis of Assisi, from 11 Pache Nostro Spiegato Dai Padre. Divine Intimacy. 111. Op cit. pp. 240, 241.

God is Listening

1. Sister Mary OCD Ed *Daily Readings with St Teresa of Avila* (Springfield Illinois, Templegate1985) p. 23.

What is God Asking of You?

1. St Teresa of Jesus OCD "The Way of Perfection" A Reading in the Proper of the Liturgy of The Hours Of The Order of The Brothers of The Blessed Virgin Mary of Mount Carmel and Of The Order of Discalced Carmelites Rome Institutum Carmelitanium 1993 p. 390.

The Darkness

1. Sister Elizabeth Ruth OCD Ed., Daily *Readings with St John of The Cross*: Ed: op cit., p. 57.

The Call of Rachel's Children

1. Carlo Coretto. Op cit., p. 82.

In Celebration Of A Life:
St. Theresa Benedicta Of The Cross

1. Wetter, Cardinal Fred rich, Josephine Koeppel OCD Trans. *Edith Stein Called to the Truth-blessed by the Cross Portrait of a Life* (Washington Province of Discalced Carmelites, Inc1998) p. 5.
2. Ibid. p. 14.
3. Ibid. p. 13.
4. Gelber L, Editor, Linssen, Michael O.C.D and Waltraut Stein Trans. *The Hidden Life: Hagiographic Essays Meditations SpiritualTexts* (Washington DC ICS Publications Institute of Carmelite Studies 1992) pp. 131-132.

The Tree Of Life

1. Catechism pp. 468-470. Op. Cit.
2. Sister Lucia "The Christian Apostolate" Magnificat Sept 2002 Vol. 4. No. 7 p. 139. Sister Lucia was a Carmelite Nun. She was the oldest of the three children to whom our Lady of Fatima appeared in 1917.